REVELATION
IN 26 LESSONS

FRANK L. COX

I0149289

GOSPEL ADVOCATE
A TRUSTED NAME SINCE 1855

Gospel Advocate Company
P.O. Box 150
Nashville, Tennessee 37202

Revelation in 26 Lessons
Gospel Advocate Reprint Library Edition, 2001

© 1956, Frank L. Cox

Published by Gospel Advocate Co.
P.O. Box 150, Nashville, TN 37202
www.gospeladvocate.com

ISBN: 0-89225-147-6

Introduction

No other book of the Bible has been subjected to more extreme treatment than the Revelation. Some have gone to the extreme of wishing it had never been written, while others have tried to explain fully all its most difficult passages.

Inspiration has pronounced a blessing on those who read and keep the things written in this marvelous book. Brother Cox has, in this book of twenty-six lessons, made a distinct contribution toward the understanding; and, therefore, toward the keeping of the things found in the Revelation.

The book deserves, and will, enjoy a wide circulation.

B. C. Goodpasture

BIBLIOGRAPHY

In the preparation of Revelation in 26 Lessons, the author made use of a number of good books, including the following:

The Pulpit Commentary
The Preacher's Homiletic Commentary
The Expositor's Bible, Milligan.
The Expositor's Greek Testament
The One Volume Bible Commentary
More Than Conquerors, Hendrikson
Gray and Adams Bible Commentary
Critical and Explanatory Commentary
Ellicott's Commentary on the Whole Bible

Not only does he make grateful acknowledgement for invaluable aid received, but also recommends these great works to the earnest student or teacher who may desire to make a more intensive study of the book of Revelation.

INDEX

Revelation in 26 Lessons

By Frank L. Cox

Revelation in 26 Lessons
Prologue

Text: Rev. 1: 1-8   **Lesson I**

The wonderful book we now open for study resembles that of Daniel and Ezekiel of the Old Testament, and belongs to a type of literature known as "Apocalyptic," a word derived from the Greek "apocalypse," which appears in the first verse of Revelation, and gives to the book its name. "Apocalypse" (or "revelation") means the uncovering of that which has been covered, the unveiling of that which has been veiled, the disclosing of that which has been concealed. (See Luke 12: 2.) The purpose of the book was to give to God's suffering people the assurance of the final overthrow of the forces of evil which oppose them and the consummation of all things at Christ's coming.

The first chapter introduces us to the entire book, and supplies us in large measure with the key by which we are to understand it. It is very necessary, therefore, that we give to chapter 1 a most studious consideration. Our attention in the initial lesson is focused on the Prologue, which includes the first eight verses of this chapter. In these verses we have the introduction to the book; the salutation; and the voice of the Eternal.

I. Introduction (Verses 1-3)

1 **The Revelation of Jesus Christ.** The book is not a revelation in which Jesus Christ is revealed; but of which he is the revealer. This is indicated in the words that follow. **Which God gave him to show unto his servants, even the things which must shortly come to pass: and he sent and signified it by his angel unto his servant John; 2 who bare witness of the word of God, and of the testimony of Jesus Christ, even of all things that he saw.** Note the four steps by which the revelation came: From God unto Jesus; from Jesus unto an angel; from an angel unto John; and from John unto God's servants. The marvelous book was committed as a sacred trust to those people who love and serve the Lord. (See Jude 3.) **3 Blessed is he that readeth, and they that hear the words of the prophecy, and keep the things that are written therein.** What a blessedness is offered! First, to him "that readeth"—the public reader, the lector. The book, or roll was meant to be read in the assembly of the saints. Second, to them "that hear." (See Psalm 1: 1, 2.) Third, to them that "keep the things," or that lay the message to heart. **For the time,** for the

beginning of fulfillment, **is at hand.** It is interesting to note that this is the first of the seven beatitudes in the book of Revelation. (For the other six see: 14: 13; 16: 15; 19: 9; 20: 6; 22: 7; and 22: 14.)

II. Salutation (Verses 4-7)

4 John, the sole survivor and representative of the apostles, **to the seven churches that are in Asia**—not the continent by that name, not even the projection known as Asia Minor, but a small province in the western extremity of Asia Minor. (See map.) There were other churches in the province, e.g., Colossae and Hierapolis. Seven churches are designated because seven is a symbolic number, representing entirety, completeness, perfection. The universal church of Christ is meant. **Grace to you and peace, from him who is and who was and who is to come; and from the seven Spirits that are before his throne**—the Holy Spirit in his perfect power and completeness; **5 and from Jesus Christ, who is the faithful witness, the firstborn of the dead, and the ruler of the kings of the earth.** The blessings bestowed upon the church are "grace" and "peace," which emanate from the self-existent, unchangeable God; from the Spirit in his perfect power; and from Jesus, the teacher, the living one, the ruler supreme· **Unto him that loveth us, and loosed us from our sins by his blood; 6 and he made us to be a kingdom, to be priests unto his God and Father: to him be the glory and the dominion for ever and ever. Amen!** The mention of the Redeemer's name awakened precious memories and brought from the heart of the aged seer an outburst of praise. But why the outburst of praise? First, because "he loveth us." We note that the tense is present, reminding us that the Redeemer's love is continuous, unbroken. You cannot remember a time when he did not love you. "Having loved his own that were in the world, he loved them unto the end." (John 13: 1.) Second, because of what he did for us. He "loosed us from our sins by his blood." In him we have obtained not only pardon for sins, but also deliverance from their power—the grip of vicious habits, the dread of penalty. "Our soul is escaped as a bird out of the snare of the fowlers: the snare is broken; and we are escaped." (Psalm 124: 7.) And third, because of what he has made of us—"To be a kingdom, to be priests." He loosed us, then ennobled us. He has given us kingly power—to rule our own passions and impulses, to rule others by wholesome influence. He has given us priestly privileges—access to the throne of grace. **7 Behold, he cometh with the clouds; and every eye shall see him, and they that pierced him; and all the tribes of the earth shall mourn over him.** With these majestic words, the theme of the book is announced: for the coming of Christ in glory is the burden of the Apocalypse. **Even so, Amen.** In this expression we have a double (Greek and Hebrew) ratification of the prophetic utterance.

III. The Voice of the Eternal (Verse 8)

8 **I am the Alpha and the Omega,** names of the first and last letters of the Greek alphabet, **saith the Lord God, who is and who was and who is to come, the Almighty.** In this passage we hear the voice of God, pointing out two characteristics of his nature. First, he is everlasting—"the Alpha and the Omega," the beginning and the ending of all things. He was on the stage when the curtain was lifted; he will be on the stage when the curtain falls. Second, he is almighty, commanding the host of heaven and earth. He is able, therefore, to overcome the foes of the church. What a consolation for the suffering saints!

From the Prologue Learn:

1. That the book we have opened to study is not a mystery, but a Revelation—something that has been uncovered. It may, therefore, be understood. Diligent study is necessary.

2. That the ultimate triumph of the people of God over the forces of evil is assured. Let them rest in peace: for Omnipotence is on their side; let them also fear: for the crown is promised only to the faithful.

3. That the Redeemer is altogether worthy of praise—because he loves us; because he "loosed us"; because he ennobles us.

4. That the saints of today are included in the seven churches— God's universal family. The great lessons of truth in the book of Revelation were intended for all Christians in every nation, in every age of the world's history.

5. That upon the man who delights in the words of this book and lays the same to heart, falls a blessedness. What an incentive to the earnest student!

Memory Selection

"Behold, he cometh with the clouds; and every eye shall see him, and they that pierced him; and all the tribes of the earth shall mourn over him. Even so, Amen." (Verse 7.)

Daily Readings

Monday: The Beatitudes of Jesus. (Matt. 5: 1-12.)
Tuesday: A Beatitude for Bible Readers. (Psalm 1: 1-6.)
Wednesday: Jesus Has Loved Us. (John 19: 1-42.)
Thursday: Jesus Has Loosed Us. (Acts 2: 1-47.)
Friday: Jesus Has Ennobled Us. (1 Cor. 6: 1-11.)
Saturday: Jesus Ascended in a Cloud. (Acts 1: 1-11.)

For Class Discussion

1. What does the word "Revelation" mean? Why was the book written?

2. Does the meaning of the word "Revelation" indicate that the book may be understood? Discuss.

3. Why is the first chapter so important?

4. What is the meaning of the word "Prologue"? (See Dictionary.)

5. Into what three divisions does the Prologue fall?

6. What do we find in the Introduction? By what four steps did the Revelation come? In verse 3, what beatitude do we have? Note the seven beatitudes in the book of Revelation.

7. What do we find in the Salutation? Who is the writer of the book? To whom was it written? Why are seven churches designated? What is symbolized by the seven churches?

8. What praise is ascribed to the Redeemer? For what three reasons?

9. Quote the memory selection. Discuss its significance.

10. In verse 8, what two characteristics of God are pointed out?

11. What practical lessons do we gather from the Prologue?

12. Give the content of each of the daily readings.

PART I

Letters to the Seven Churches

(Rev. 1: 9-3: 22)

THE FIRST VISION

Text: Rev. 1: 9-22   Lesson II

We come now to the letters addressed to the seven churches. This section of the book is introduced with a vision of the glorified Christ. That John should have been favored with such a vision is in harmony with what had often been granted to other spokesmen of the Lord—to Moses at the burning bush (Ex. 3), to Isaiah in the temple (Isa. 6), to Jeremiah when called to the prophetic office (Jer. 1), to Ezekiel by the river Chebar (Ezek. 1), and to Saul of Tarsus on the Damascus Road (Acts 9). These visions were designed to qualify and to equip those great personalities for the services the Lord had for them to do. Upon the beloved John had fallen a responsibility of major importance. How fitting, therefore, that the Christ of glory should appear unto him at the beginning of his undertaking!

In the lesson text we have a sublime charge, a glorious vision, and the charge repeated.

I. A Sublime Charge (Verses 9-11)

9 I John, your brother and partaker with you in the tribulation and kingdom and patience which are in Jesus. "It is no longer the apostle, the authoritative messenger of God, who speaks; it is one who occupies the same ground as other members of the church, and is bound to them by the strong deep tie of common sorrow. The aged and honored evangelist, 'the disciple whom Jesus loved,' is one with them, bears the same burden, drinks the same cup, and has no higher consolation than they may have." As their brother in the Lord and their fellow citizen in the kingdom, he was a partaker with them in all their sorrows and trials and tribulations. Like them, he had known the bitterness of persecution. **Was in the isle that is called Patmos, for the word of God and the testimony of Jesus.** The apostle was an exile on this small, rocky, barren island—about ten miles long and six miles wide—off the southwest coast of Asia Minor. It was in consequence of his fidelity to the word of God that he had been transported to this lonely place. Though restricted to a small spot upon the earth, he was to penetrate the wide realms of heaven. Other great men of God had seen visions while in exile. In exile, Jacob saw God at Bethel; in exile, Moses saw God at the burning bush; in exile, Elijah heard "a sound of gentle stillness"; in exile, Ezekiel "saw visions of God" by the river Chebar; in exile, Daniel saw the "Ancient of Days." 10 **I was in the Spirit,** a state of spiritual ecstasy, **on the Lord's day,** the Lord's resurrection day, the first day of the week. (See Matt. 28: 1-10; Acts 20: 7.) **And I heard behind me a great voice, as of a trumpet,** strong and distinct, 11 **Saying, What thou seest,** in the course of this vision, **write in a book and send it to the seven churches: unto Ephesus, and unto Smyrna, and unto Pergamum, and unto Thyatira, and unto Sardis, and unto Philadelphia, and unto Laodicea.** Thus, upon John fell an obligation most solemn. He was to observe, to "write," and to "send." The voices and visions on Patmos were not intended for John alone, but for God's universal church. With a map of the province of Asia before us, we observe that these seven cities form an irregular circle and are mentioned in the order in which a messenger on circuit might visit them, going north from Ephesus to Smyrna and Pergamum, then east to Thyatira, and southward to Sardis, Philadelphia and Laodicea.

II. Christ of Glory (Verses 12-16)

12 **And I turned to see the voice that spake with me.** In this place, as in Gen. 3: 8, "the voice" is put for the speaker. **And having turned I saw seven golden candlesticks.** They were not united into one as in the Tabernacle; but seven distinct, independent lamps. 13 **And in the midst of the candlesticks one like unto a son of man.** This is the Lord Jesus in the very heart of the church, of which he is the head and sustainer. Note the description that John gave. **Clothed with a garment down to the foot**—a priestly garment, reminding us that Jesus is our great high priest. "Enough is said to indicate that the son of man claims and fulfils the office which was assigned to the children of Aaron; that he blesses the people in God's name; that he stands as their representative before the Father." (Maurice.) **And girt about at the breast with a golden girdle**—a kingly garment, reminding us that Jesus is our ruler. (See Isa. 22: 21.) **And his head and his hair were white as white wool, white as snow.** From the priestly and kingly garments of the glorified Christ, John passes to Christ himself. The color indicates his purity, his glory, his eternity. (Read Dan. 7: 9.) What the apostle had seen on the Mount of Transfiguration as an outflashing of his glory (Matt. 17), he now sees on Patmos as an abiding condition of the Christ. **And his eyes were as a flame of fire**—searching, penetrating. Nothing escapes his notice. (See Jer. 17: 10.) 15 **And his feet like unto**

burnished brass, as if it had been refined in a furnace. Like fine brass, his feet were strong and durable—able to crush all opposition. (See 1 Cor. 15: 25-28.) And his voice as the voice of many waters, i.e., resounding, musical, powerful. Perhaps the roar of the sea was in the ears of the lonely man as he was writing. 16 And he had in his right hand seven stars, reminding us that Jesus is the possessor and upholder of his light-bearers, or ministers. By his grace, he sustains them. And out of his mouth proceedeth a sharp two-edged sword. This is his word, sharp and incisive. (Heb. 4: 12.) And his countenance was as the sun shineth in his strength. His face was majestic, radiant with glory. Jesus is "the sun of righteousness" and "the light of the world."

III. The Charge Repeated (Verses 17-20)

17 And when I saw him, I fell at his feet as one dead. With this stroke of the pen, John describes his own reaction to the wonderful vision. By the appearance of the Christ of glory, he was overwhelmed. "It is in mercy to us that so much of the glory of the savior is concealed from us. We could no more bear to see it in its fulness than our eyes could bear to gaze on the splendor of the noonday sun. Hence it is necessary for us that as yet we should see only through a glass darkly." And he laid his right hand upon me, as an expression of divine compassion. This wasn't the first time that the beloved disciple had felt the touch of this kind and mighty hand. (See Matt. 17: 7.) Saying, Fear not. This indicates that John was terrified. Till rid of fear, he was unfit to receive instruction. After the tender touch and the gentle admonition, the Master gave utterance to a great declaration, the very epitome of the gospel. (See 1 Cor. 15: 1-8.) I am the first and the last, 18 and the Living one; and I was dead, and behold, I am alive for evermore, and I have the keys of death and of Hades. These majestic words contain four disclosures concerning the glory of the Lord. First, that he is eternal—"the first and the last." He has always been; he is ever to be. He is as eternal as God himself; for he is God. Second, that he was crucified. "I was (or, became) dead." Into this painful experience he entered by means of his incarnation. (See John 1: 1, 14.) As a man, he died. "He died for our sins." Third, that he was victorious in death. He is "the Living one" and he is "alive for evermore." No longer is he in the grip of death. Never again shall he know its pain or shame. Fourth, that the power of life and death are in his hand. "I have the keys of death and Hades." Hades is the realm of departed spirits, death the gate thereto. Over both Christ has supreme control. The keys

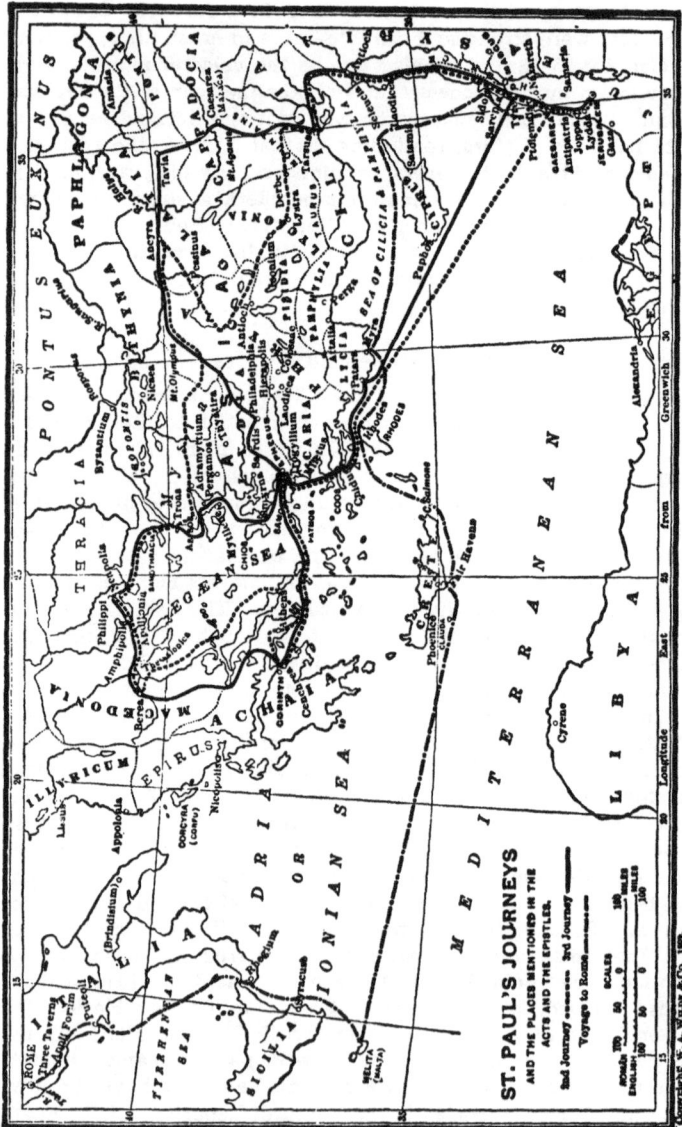

ST. PAUL'S JOURNEYS

AND THE PLACES MENTIONED IN THE
ACTS AND THE EPISTLES.

2nd Journey ········· 3rd Journey ▬▬▬▬
Voyage to Rome ▬▬▬▬

SCALES

Copyright, W. & A. K. Johnston & Co., 1889.

— 8 —

are in his hand. The spacious world unseen is his. Under his power are all departed dead. (See John 11: 25.) Having conquered the death monster for himself, he is able to conquer him for all. 19 **Write therefore the things which thou sawest, and the things which are, and the things which shall come to pass hereafter; 20 the mystery of the seven stars which thou sawest in thy right hand, and the seven golden candlesticks. The seven stars are the angels of the seven churches: and the seven candlesticks are seven churches.** In these words the Master repeated the solemn charge in verse 11 and gave an explanation. The stars are the angels, or ministers. The candlesticks are the churches. This reminds us that the function of a minister and a church is to illuminate, to enlighten the world in reference to God's will.

From This Chapter Portion Learn:

1. That the good things we derive from divine revelation are not ours to keep or to hoard, but to share or to divide.
2. That Christ is in the midst of the churches to inspect, to encourage, to rebuke, to save.
3. That gospel ministers are stars, the churches candlesticks. They are to reflect the light of the Sun of Righteousness to a world that.lies in darkness—the darkness of sin, of ignorance, of despair. (See Mark 16: 15, 16.)

Memory Selection

"I am the first and the last, and the Living one; and I was dead, and behold, I am alive for evermore, and I have the keys of death and Hades." (Verses 17, 18.)

Daily Readings

Monday: The Great Commission. (Matt. 28: 16-20; Mark 16: 9-20; Luke 24: 44-49.)
Tuesday: The Glorified Christ. (Matt. 17: 1-8; Luke 9: 28-36.)
Wednesday: Moses at the Burning Bush. (Ex. 2.)
Thursday: Isaiah in the Temple. (Isa. 6.)
Friday: The Vision of Daniel. (Dan. 10.)
Saturday: Ezekiel at the River Chebar. (Ezek. 1.)

For Class Discussion
1. To what section of the book do we now come?
2. With what is this section introduced?
3. Mention the names of some men of God to whom visions came? Why were these visions given?
4. Into how many parts may the lesson text be divided? Name the parts.
5. How does John, the writer, introduce himself to the readers?
6. Where was John when he wrote the book? Describe this place. Locate it on a map. On what day did the vision appear? What charge came to the aged apostle? On a map, point out the seven cities mentioned.
7. Describe John's vision of Christ. What was his reaction to this vision?
8. Repeat the memory selection and discuss its significance.
9. Why do you suppose the charge was repeated?
10. In verse 20, what explanation is given?
11. What practical lessons may be gathered from the lesson text?
12. Point out the relation between the daily readings and the lesson text.

LETTER TO THE CHURCH IN EPHESUS

Text: Rev. 2: 1-7   **Lesson III**

Ephesus was not only the capital of the province of Asia, but the city of prime importance in all Asia Minor, a splendid city, and the principal emporium of trade in the East. It was called "one of the eyes of Asia," the other being Smyrna, forty miles to the north. The city stood on the south of a plain about five miles in length, east to west, and three miles in breadth, washed by an arm of the Aegean Sea. The crowning glory of Ephesus was the temple of Diana, one of the seven wonders of the ancient world, whose magnificence has been a marvel even unto our day. "It glittered in brilliant beauty at the head of the harbor, and it was said that the sun saw nothing in his course more magnificent than Diana's temple. Made of purest marble, upon splendid foundations, which in that marshy ground were at once costly and essential, it confronted the mariner immediately at the landing-place."

The church in Ephesus was probably the foremost of the seven. From the facts we gather, we conclude that it was founded by Paul. (Acts 18, 19 and 20; 1 Tim. 1: 3, 4.) There the apostle lived and labored for three years. There he preached the gospel effectively, worked miracles, witnessed the bonfire of evil books, and saw people turn from darkness to light, from sin to salvation. There the eloquent Apollos, an Alexandrian Jew, had labored, also learned the way of the Lord more perfectly. In later years, Timothy made his home in Ephesus, and so did the beloved John. Two apostolic letters were written to the Ephesian church—one by Paul, the other by John.

The letter before us is brief, but meaningful. Found therein are words of commendation, of condemnation, of exhortation, of warning, and of encouragement.

Salutation (Verse 1)

1 **To the angel of the church in Ephesus write.** The letter was addressed to "the angel (messenger, or minister) of the church" to be read by him to the assembly. **These things saith he that holdeth the seven stars in his right hand, he that walketh in the midst of the seven golden candlesticks.** Though written by the hand of John, the letter was dictated by the Lord Jesus. Of him a two-point description is given. First, he holds the stars or ministers in his right hand—within his grasp. He sustains them, protects them, directs them. To the loyal light-bearer, this is a thought most assuring. (See Matt. 10: 30; Acts 18: 8, 10.) Second, he walks in the midst of the candlesticks or churches. The glorified Christ is present in the churches to inspect, to warn, to encourage, to condemn, to reward. Having been introduced to the head of the church, we are ready to consider the contents of his message.

I. Commendation (Verses 2, 3, 6)

2 **I know thy works.** Having eyes "as a flame of fire," he saw their activities. He knew all about them. Nothing good or bad had escaped his notice. (See Heb. 4: 12, 13.) **And thy toil and patience, and that thou canst not bear evil men, and didst try them that call themselves apostles, and they are not, and didst find them false; 3 and thou hast patience and didst bear for my name's sake, and hast not grown weary.** With this group of Christians, three things were right. First, the life was right. Prominent in the lives of these people were active virtues, also passive virtues. They had labored unto weariness. They had "learned to labor and to wait." Without complaint they had endured fierce opposition, all for the sake of Jesus' name. Second, the discipline was right. They had set themselves against "evil men." It is right to bear with a weak brother, but not with a false one. (See Rom. 15: 1; 2 John 10, 11.) They had tested the teachings of self-styled apostles and found them false. See Acts 20: 28-30.) 6 **But this thou hast,** to thy credit, **that**

thou hatest the works of the Nicolaitans, which I also hate. Christians should hate the things that the Lord hates, also love the things he loves. The Nicolaitans turned "the grace of God into lasciviousness," contending that idol worship and the sensuality connected therewith were matters of indifference. (See Jude 4; Rom. 6: 1, 2.) And third, the doctrine was right. The purity of their doctrine is brought to light in the sternness of the discipline they exercised: for only a people who hold to the New Testament teaching will silence false teachers and take a positive stand against immoral conduct.

II. Condemnation (Verse 4)

4 **But**—what an ominous transition word! A fly was in the ointment. **I have this against thee, that thou didst leave thy first love.** The church suffered only one ailment, but that was a serious one— a heart-ailment. While they hated the things the Lord hated, they did not love all the things he loved. How warm and genuine was their love when they were joined to the Bridegroom in spiritual wedlock! But they had departed from the love. And when love wanes, every virtue is in danger. This is true because love is at the root of every virtue. (See 1 Cor. 13.) But, let us ask, what was the cause of this waning love? It was an attachment to the present evil world. Love for the world will stifle one's love for the Lord. (See Matt. 24: 12; 1 John 2: 15.) No heart is big enough to love the Lord and the world at the same time.

III. Exhortation and Warning (Verse 5)

5 **Remember therefore whence thou art fallen, and repent and do the first works.** When these people grew cold at heart, they suffered a relapse; they fell. Christ said so—"thou art fallen." In an effort to revive their fading love, he called three things into action. First, their memory, "the lever of repentance." The memory of brighter days and a better land caused a wayward nation to weep by the willows (Psalm 137), and a prodigal son to say in sorrow, "I will arise and go to my father." (Luke 15.) Second, their will— "And repent." Repentance involves the will, the executive faculty of the mind. When they left their first love, they experienced a major setback in spiritual growth; and now a change was sorely needed. Coldness of heart is a sinful condition, and the only remedy is repentance. And third, their bodies. "Do the first works," that is, the works prompted by their first love. (See Eph. 1: 15, 16.) "In Christ Jesus neither circumcision availeth anything, nor uncircumcision; but faith working through love." (Paul.) **Or else I come to**

thee, and will move thy candlestick out of its place, except thou repent. The candlestick is the church; so the removal of the Ephesian church was threatened. In spite of the purity of her doctrine and the sternness of her discipline, the church was threatened with extinction. Doctrinal purity is important, and discipline is important, but these things alone will not save the church from extinction. Without the presence of brotherly love, no congregation can long exist. Coldness of heart will remove the best things of life.

IV. Encouragement (Verse 7)

7 He that hath an ear, let him hear what the Spirit saith to the churches. To him that overcometh, to him will I give to eat of the tree of life, which is in the Paradise (garden) of God. These words, which bring the letter to a close, carry a twofold admonition. First, to hear the words of the Spirit. Each of the seven churches received the same admonition, an indication of its importance. The heart that is open to God's word is soon filled with God's grace, including the grace of love, which they had lost. (See Matt. 11: 15; 13: 9, 43; Mark 4: 9, 23; Luke 8: 8; 14: 35.) Second, to overcome the world. They were not to conform their lives to the world (Rom. 12: 2), but to meet the world in conflict. To the victor is promised the tree of life. This life-giving tree, which thrived in Eden, was forfeited by an act of disobedience; now, through a life of obedience, it may be regained.

Though the letter is addressed to a congregation, the concluding verse, with its exhortation and promise, is addressed to the individual Christian—"he that hath an ear, let him hear" and "to him that overcometh, to him will I give," etc. Each Christian must hear for himself, overcome for himself. The congregation may be removed, yet if he hears and overcomes, he shall survive. The congregation may be crowned with life eternal, yet if he is overcome, he shall lose his reward.

From This Letter We Learn:

1. That Christ is omniscient. He knows all about us—our words, our deeds, even the secret emotions of the heart. A thought most sobering!

2. That Christ seems more intent on finding the good than the evil in the lives of his people. He sees the good before he sees the evil. He finds the good as a matter of delight, but the evil as a painful necessity. Let the Christian imitate the Christ.

3. That a Christian should hate everything that Christ hates, and love everything that Christ loves. (See Prov. 6: 16-19; Matt. 5: 1-12.)

4. That when a Christian departs from love, he departs from God: "for God is love." (1 John 4: 8.)

5. That the Christian who has left his first love, has fallen, and stands in need of repentance. Christ calls upon him to repent.

6. That without the spirit of brotherly love, a congregation is doomed to extinction, no matter how pure her doctrine or stern her discipline.

Memory Selection

"I have this against thee, that thou didst leave thy first love. Remember therefore whence thou art fallen, and repent and do the first works." (Verses 4, 5a.)

Daily Readings

Monday: Founding of the Ephesian Church. (Acts 19, 20.)
Tuesday: The Blessings of Redemption. (Eph. 1: 1-23.)
Wednesday: "You Did He Make Alive." (Eph. 2: 1-22.)
Thursday: "I Bow My Knees." (Eph. 3: 1-21.)
Friday: "Walk Worthily." (Eph. 4: 1-32.)
Saturday: "The Whole Armor of God." (Eph. 6: 1-24.)

For Class Discussion

1. What can you say of the city of Ephesus?
2. Give a brief historical sketch of the church in Ephesus.
3. In verse 1, what two-point description is given of the Lord Jesus?
4. What three things were right with this church?
5. What was wrong with the church? Discuss the seriousness of this state.
6. What did the Lord exhort them to do?
7. What threat did he hold out before them? What is the significance of the removal of the candlestick? Can a congregation long exist without love?
8. What two admonitions are found in the last verse?
9. What practical lessons can we learn from this letter? Discuss.
10. Point out the relation between the daily readings with the lesson in hand.

LETTER TO THE CHURCH IN SMYRNA
Text: Rev. 2: 8-11   **Lesson IV**

A messenger, departing from Ephesus for the other churches of this group, would naturally go first to Smyrna, about forty miles north on an arm of the Aegean Sea. Smyrna ranked as one of the most beautiful cities of the province and was often called "the ornament of Asia." Trench speaks of it "as one of the finest and noblest of Iona, being most favorably placed upon the coast to command the trade of the Levant, which equally in old and modern times it has enjoyed."

Concerning the establishment of the church in Smyrna, we have no direct information. It was probably established by the apostle Paul during his third evangelistic journey, 53-56 A.D. In Acts 19: 10 we are informed that the teaching of the apostle in the school of Tyrannus in the city of Ephesus "continued for the space of two years; so that all they that dwelt in Asia heard the word of the Lord, both Jews and Greeks." It is not improbable that people from Smyrna heard, believed and were baptized in Ephesus during Paul's sojourn there.

This little letter, the shortest of the seven, abounds in beauty. After the greeting or salutation, we come to words of praise, words of prophecy, and words of promise.

Salutation (Verse 8)

8 **And to the angel of the church in Smyrna write.** The great Polycarp, a disciple of John and a martyr for Christ, was a bishop of the congregation and perhaps "the angel" to whom the letter was addressed. John was the writer, but the words he wrote were the words of Christ, who is portrayed in language calculated to console the saints in this city in their great sorrow. **These things saith the first and the last,** "the Alpha and Omega" of the Christian dispensation, the author and finisher of our faith. **Who was dead, and lived again.** In this little expression is couched an epitome of the gospel . The death and resurrection are the two great divisions of the work of the Lord Jesus on our behalf. (See 1 Cor. 15: 1-4.) Christ died to live again; you die and you shall live again. What a fine thought to encourage a people who were to be called upon to die for their faith!

I. Words of Praise (Verse 9)

9 **I know thy tribulation, and thy poverty (but thou art rich),**

and the blasphemy of them that say they are Jews, and they are not, but are a synagogue of Satan. They were commended for their heroic endurance. Smyrna was a suffering church, and against the same no word of reproach was spoken. Had these saints been refined by suffering? Their tribulation came in two forms. First, in the despoiling of their goods. The ruthless hand of persecution had reduced them to dire poverty. (See Heb. 10: 34.) Though they had lost their material possessions, they retained their spiritual wealth: for the Savior said, "Thou art rich." It is interesting to note the contrast between the church in Smyrna and the church in Laodicea. One was poor in the world's goods, but rich before God; the other was rich in the world's goods, but poor before God. "There are both poor rich-men, and rich poor-men in God's sight." (Trench.) Second, in the blasphemy (insult and slander) they suffered. This opposition came from the bigoted Jewish party in whose synagogue the Christians likely worshipped. They slandered the name of the Lord by calling him "the hanged one." At the martyrdom of Polycarp some years later, "they joined the heathens in clamoring for his being cast to the lions; and when there was an obstacle to this, for his being burnt alive; with their hands they carried logs for the pile." The saints in Smyrna must have been godly in life, else they would not have drawn such opposition.

II. Words of Prophecy (Verse 10a)

10a **Fear not the things which thou art about to suffer: behold, the devil is about to cast some of you into prison, that ye may be tried; and ye shall have tribulation ten days.** Other trials and tribulations were to come, perhaps more severe than any they had known. In store for them were the pain and shame of imprisonment, perhaps death itself. But they were to face these things with calm courage, trusting in the mightly arm of the Lord. The author of these things was "the devil," "the accuser of our brethren." (Rev. 10: 12.) Doubtless, he would act through the agency of the local Jewish party. The duration of the persecution would be "ten days," a short but definite period of time. For the child of God, all evil is temporary. (Job. 3: 17; 2 Cor. 4: 17.) This fact is frequently urged as a motive for patient endurance. (See Isa. 26: 30; 54: 8; Matt. 24: 22; 2 Cor. 4: 13; 1 Pet. 1: 6.) For the joy set before him, the captain of our salvation endured the cross, despising the shame. (Heb. 12: 2.) The fact that the Lord knows all that we suffer for him should serve at least three purposes. It should cause us to seek his help. It should inspire us with courage invincible. And it should clothe us with deepest humility.

III. Words of Promise (Verses 10b, 11)

10b **Be thou faithful unto death, and I will give thee the crown of life.** 11 **He that hath an ear, let him hear what the Spirit saith to the churches. He that overcometh shall not be hurt of the second death.** In this language two precious promises are pledged, not only to the suffering saints in ancient Smyrna, but also to people of like character in every age of the world.

The first promise is positive in nature. "I will give thee the crown of life." Christ is the gracious giver. "I [Christ] will give." Because he is the "Prince of Life" and the conqueror of death, he is abundantly able to bestow the gift of life. The metaphor "crown" is employed in various places in sacred writ. Paul speaks of his own personal hope of "the crown of righteousness." (2 Tim. 4: 8.) James speaks of "the crown of life, which the Lord promised to them that love him." (James 1: 12.) Peter speaks of "the crown of glory that fadeth not away." (1 Pet. 5: 4.) Paul also speaks of "the crown incorruptible." (1 Cor. 9: 25.) All of these expressions mean substantially the same thing, namely, that God will reward his people with life incorruptible and full of glory. But let us note the condition upon which the crown is promised: "Be thou faithful unto death." Be faithful until you die. More than that, be faithful though you have to pay for your fidelity with your life. There is something more precious than life itself. It was said of Daniel that "he was faithful, neither was there any error or fault in him." (Dan. 4: 4.) It was said of Judah that he "ruleth with God, and is faithful with the Holy One." (Hos. 11: 12.) The apostle Paul spoke of Timothy as "my beloved and faithful child in the Lord." (1 Cor. 4: 17.) He also called Tychicus, "the beloved brother and faithful minister in the Lord." (Eph. 6: 21.) It was said of the Savior that he "was faithful to him that appointed him, as also was Moses in all his house." (Heb. 3: 2.) And the apostle Peter admonishes us most earnestly to commit our souls "in well-doing unto a faithful Creator." (1 Pet. 4: 19.)

The second promise is negative—immunity from punishment of the most fearful form. "He that overcometh shall not be hurt of the second death." The corresponding expression, "the first death," does not appear. One is the death of the body, to which the Christians in Smyrna must yield; the other is the death of the soul, from which the crown of life secures them. Unto them the Prince of Life seems to say, "The hand of injustice may strike once, but that is all. They may take your goods, slander your good name, blaspheme the name of your Savior, imprison you, burn you, feed you to the lions, but they cannot inflict the second death. Keep yourselves until death; I will keep you after death." (See Rev. 20: 14, 15; 21: 8.)

From This Letter Learn:

1. That unto the saints who suffer, Christ comes with words of consolation. "I am the Alpha and the Omega. I was dead, but live again. Lo, I am with you."

2. That the tribulation through which we are passing is a flame of fire which consumes the impurities within and fits us for a higher habitation. Some day, if not now, we shall thank God for our fiery trials. (See James 1: 2-4.)

3. That it is better by far to be rich in grace and poor in earthly goods, than to be poor in grace and rich in earthly goods.

4. That it is better to suffer injury than it is to inflict injury. The blessing of the Savior does not fall upon the persecutor, but upon those people who are persecuted for righteousness' sake. (See Matt. 5: 10-12.)

5. That the higher the tone of the Christian life, the more likely it is to draw opposition or hostility. It isn't the lukewarm Christian, but the zealous Christian that Satan pursues. (See 2 Tim. 3: 12; Acts 14: 22.)

6. That the suffering of a Christian is confined altogether to the life that now is. He shall not feel the pangs of the second death—"the lake that burneth with fire and brimstone."

Memory Selection

"Be thou faithful unto death, and I will give thee the crown of life." (Verse 10b.)

Daily Readings

Monday: The Suffering Servant. (Isa. 53: 1-12.)
Tuesday: In the Shadows. (Matt. 26: 1-35.)
Wednesday: In Gethsemane. (Matt. 26: 36-46.)
Thursday: The Betrayal, Denial, and Trial. (Matt. 26: 47-27: 31.)
Friday: The Crucifixion. (Matt. 27: 32-66.)
Saturday: The Resurrection. (Matt. 28: 1-20.)

For Class Discussion

1. Locate the city of Smyrna. Which direction is it from Ephesus? (See map.)

2. Describe the city.

3. What can you say concerning the establishment of the church in Smyrna?

4. How is Jesus portrayed in the salutation? Show that the language in verse 8 is calculated to console the saints in sorrow.

5. What words of praise are found in verse 9? Do we find any words of blame in this letter?

6. In what two forms did the tribulation come?

7. What prophecy concerning the saints in Smyrna do we have in verse 10? How were they to face the persecution? Who was the author of the persecution? What would be the duration of the persecution?

8. What promises are found in verses 10 and 11? Which promise is positive in nature? Negative?

9. What practical lessons do we gather from this letter?

10. Point out the relation between the lesson text and the daily readings.

LETTER TO THE CHURCH IN PERGAMUM

Text: Rev. 2: 12-17   **Lesson V**

Some sixty miles north of Smyrna, near the site of ancient Troy, was the city of Pergamum. It was situated three miles north of the river Caicus, about fifteen from the sea. (See map.) The city, first mentioned by Xenophon, rose to prominence and magnificence under Attalus, a friend of the Romans (241-197 B.C.), and his son Eumenes (196-159 B.C.). Its library of 200,000 volumes (rolls) was second only to that of Alexandria; but Mark Anthony moved it to Egypt and gave it to Cleopatra who, in turn, incorporated it in the great Alexandrian library. Parchment gets its name from Pergamum, for the reason that it was invented in that city. Pergamum was a stronghold of anti-Christian idolatry. This fact has considerable bearing on our lesson. The city now goes by the name of Bergamo, but has been reduced to comparative decay. It has "extensive remains of a palace, an amphitheatre, triumphal arches, and bridges, intermixed with huts, burial-grounds, mosques, and khans, or Turkish inns. It has a very degraded population of about 12,000, chiefly Turks."

Concerning the origin of the church in Pergamum, we have no information. Perhaps, some unnamed disciples, converted under the preaching of Peter or Paul or John in other places, came to this pagan city and set in motion the activities which resulted in the establishment of the congregation.

The letter begins with a salutation; continues with words of approval, words of comfort, and words of admonition; and concludes with words of promise.

Salutation (Verse 12)

12 **And to the angel of the church in Pergamum write: These things saith he that hath the sharp two-edged sword.** Christ approaches this congregation as the bearer of "the sharp two-edged sword," which is the word of God. (Eph. 6: 17; Heb. 4: 12; Rev. 1: 16.) Being "sharp," it penetrates the smallest opening, pricks the heart, lays bare the secrets. Being "two-edged," it cuts two ways —convicts man of sin, also of righteousness; converts some and condemns others; saves all who accept it and slays all who reject it. In view of conditions that prevailed in this congregation, we can understand why the Master came with such a sword.

I. Words of Approval (Verse 13)

13 **I know where thou dwellest, even where Satan's throne is.** This was a church with an evil environment. In that city Satan was enthroned—pagan religion in numerous forms prevailed. Standing in Pergamum were temples erected to Zeus, Apollo, Dionysius, Aphrodite, and Aesculapius, which was the god of healing symbolized by a serpent. Connected with the worship of these idols was sensuality in forms most degrading. "Satan's throne" or power was a seducing power, enticing unstable souls into pagan worship with its immoral rites. It was also a persecuting power. When pagans failed to seduce a Christian, they made life very unpleasant for him. **And thou holdest fast my name.** Though the environment was evil, they were true to the Savior. How wonderful and how meaningful is the name of Christ! "His name shall be called Immanuel, God with us." "This is the name whereby he shall be called, The Lord our Righteousness." In that precious name is found the doctrine of Christianity.

> "There is no name so sweet on earth,
> No name so sweet in heaven,
> The name before his wondrous birth
> To Christ the Savior given."

And didst not deny my faith. Paraphrase: "Thou hast not been ashamed of me; thou hast boldly maintained my cause; thou hast not been afraid to acknowledge me, even in the presence of my bitter foes." (See Rom. 1: 16.) **Even in the days of Antipas my witness, my faithful one, who was killed among you, where Satan dwelleth.** Brother Antipas is given as an individual example of the loyalty of these Christians. Rather than worship an idol, he gave up his life. According to a legendary story, he was shut up in a brazen bull, and ended his life in thanksgiving and prayer.

II. Words of Reproof (Verses 14, 15)

14 **But I have a few things against thee, because thou hast there some that hold the teaching of Balaam, who taught Balak to cast a stumblingblock before the children of Israel, to eat things sacrificed to idols, and to commit fornication. 15 So hast thou also some that hold the teaching of the Nicolaitans in like manner.** Some Christians in Pergamum pleased the Lord and won his loving approval; others displeased him and received his reproof. With "the sharp two-edged sword" he laid bare their sins. First, evil doctrines were taught—the doctrine of Balaam and the doctrine of the Nicolaitans. The Balaamites, like Balaam of old, debased spiritual gifts to purposes most vile, and, by so doing, became a snare or stumblingblock to others. (See Num. 22, 23 and 24.) The Nicolaitans, as we learned in a previous lesson, taught that the freedom of the gospel lifts men above the moral law, conferring license to worship idols and to commit the vilest of sins. The practical results of the two doctrines seem to be about the same. Second, False teachers were tolerated—"thou hast some," etc. Though some members of the congregation did not teach the grievous error, they were guilty of laxity or false kindness toward the errorists. The stern discipline, prominent in the church in Ephesus, was lacking in Pergamum.

III. Words of Admonition (Verse 16)

16 **Repent therefore; or else I come to thee quickly, and I will make war against them with the sword of my mouth.** Religious error and the attitude of compromise called for earnest admonition and drastic action. The congregation was given the choice of two courses. The first was repentance. Instead of being lax toward the errorists, the congregation was called upon to exercise discipline. (See 1 Cor. 5: 4, 5.) The second, or allow the errorists to be exposed to the wrath of God. Laxity or the compromising attitude exposes sinners to an alternative more serious than discipline. The toleration of sin is false kindness. An angel of divine wrath with drawn sword stands before false teachers. He who does not heed

the warning will be slain. (See Num. 22: 21-34; 31: 8.) "It is a fearful thing to fall into the hands of the living God." (Heb. 10: 21.)

IV. Words of Promise (Verse 17)

17 **He that hath an ear, let him hear what the Spirit saith to the churches.** How important it is to have an open heart, a. listening ear—an ear attuned to the voice of the Infinite! Without a listening ear, no one shall see salvation. **To him that overcometh,** the world, the flesh, and the devil, **to him will I give of the hidden manna, and I will give him a white stone, and upon the stone a new name written, which no one knoweth but he that receiveth it.** In these beautiful words, three blessings are assured the one who hears and overcomes. First, "The hidden manna." On their journey through a dreary desert to the land of promise, the children of Israel were sustained by manna; for them a table was spread in the wilderness. On his journey through a wilderness of trials and temptations, the Christian is nourished by Jesus himself—"manna" from above, "the bread of life." (John 6.) He is that "hidden" or unseen influence that sustains every pilgrim on the way to "the fair and happy land." Second, "a white stone." The full significance of this metaphor is not so clear; but it undoubtedly is a token of divine justification or favor which admits the one receiving it into the secret place of the Most High. Third, "a new name." A new name indicates an advancement in life—Abram, Abraham; Jacob, Israel. (See Rev. 3: 12; 22: 4.) Perhaps, a more intimate relationship with the Father is implied. "White" and "new," as Trench reminds us, are key-words in the book of Revelation. It is natural that they should be. "White is the livery of heaven, where white robes, white clouds, white horses, and white thrones abound. . . . And 'new' is almost as frequent as 'white' in the book which tells of a new heaven, and a new earth, in which is the new Jerusalem; where the inhabitants have a new name, and sing a new song, and where all things are made new."

From This Letter Learn:

1. That we can live the true life in any locality, "even where Satan's throne is." In the house of Potiphar, Joseph kept himself pure. (Gen. 39.) While in the power of a heathen ruler, Daniel did not defile himself. (Dan. 4.) There were saints in Caesar's household. (Phil. 4: 22.)

2. That it is right to love the sinner, no matter how vile; but it is never right to sanction his sins or condone his error. To compromise with error is to encourage the errorist and the wavering

souls he may be leading on to perdition. Toleration of evil is false kindness.

3. That the promises of God are not pledged to the Christian that is overcome, but to the Christian that overcomes. By fervent prayer, by diligent service, by daily Bible study, by a constant attendance of the meetings of the church, by always "looking to Jesus," a Christian can overcome evil, no matter how powerful its influence.

4. That a Christian "may live in the very abode of Satan, and within hearing of damnable doctrines; yet if he overcomes the wiles of Satan, and listens to the Spirit rather than to the seducers, he shall eat of the hidden manna which restores the spirit that the flesh-pots of Egypt weakened. He shall have the white stone of absolution, the true spiritual emancipation, which the Balaamite and Nicolaitan emancipation counterfeited."—Maurice.

Memory Selection

"He that hath an ear, let him hear what the Spirit saith to the churches. To him that overcometh, to him will I give of the hidden manna, and I will give him a white stone, and upon the stone a new name written, which no one knoweth but he that receiveth it." (Verse 17.)

Daily Readings

Monday: An Idol Is Nothing. (Psalm 135: 1-21.)
Tuesday: Guard Yourselves from Idols. (1 John 5: 1-21.)
Wednesday: Joseph in Potiphar's House. (Gen. 39: 1-23.)
Thursday: Daniel in the Hand of a Heathen. (Dan. 1: 1-21.)
Friday: Saints in Caesar's Household. (Phil. 4: 1-23.)
Saturday: The Whole Armor of God. (Eph. 6: 1-23.)

For Class Discussion

1. Locate the city of Pergamum. How far is it from Ephesus? Smyrna? the sea?
2. Give a historical sketch of the city.
3. What can you say concerning the founding of the church there?
4. Comment on the salutation in verse 12.

5. What attitude or condition in the church received the Lord's approval?

6. What did he hold against them?

7. In verse 16, what admonition and warning do we have?

8. In verse 17, what three promises are made? Upon what condition?

9. What important lessons are suggested in the letter?

10. Quote the memory selection.

11. Report to the class your findings in the daily readings. Point out the relation of these selections with the assignment.

LETTER TO THE CHURCH IN THYATIRA

Text: Rev. 2: 18-29   **Lesson VI**

Thyatira—never a city of much note—was on a highway between Pergamum and Sardis. It had been known as Pelopia and Euhippa; but when Seleucus Nicator colonized it with Greeks (301-281 B. C.), he gave it the name of Thyatira. The inhabitants of this ancient city were widely known for their skill in dyeing purple. We recall that Lydia, the first convert to Christ in Philippi, was "a seller of purple, of the city of Thyatira." (Acts 16: 11-15.)

It is not improbable that this Christian lady played an important part in the founding of the church in her native city. Trench suggests that "she who had gone forth for a while, to buy and get gain, when she returned brought back with her far richer merchandise than she looked to gain."

The letter to the church in Smyrna is the shortest; but the letter to the church in Thyatira is the longest of the seven. It begins with the salutation, continues with language of commendation and condemnation, and closes with language of encouragement.

Salutation (Verse 18)

18 **And to the angel of the church in Thyatira write: These things saith the Son of God, who hath his eyes like a flame of fire,** or eyes all-penetrating. The eyes of the Lord are his infinite wisdom. He is the all-wise inspector. (See Psalm 11: 4; Zech. 4: 10.) **And his feet are like unto burnished brass,** that is, strong and durable. The Son of God is able to crush under foot all evil his eyes may discover.

I. Commendation (Verse 19)

19 **I know thy works, and thy love and faith and ministry and patience, and that thy last works are more than the first.** According

—24—

to custom, the Son of God informs them that he knows their works —life and conduct in general. Nothing escapes his attention. He had discovered their excellent qualities; now he specifies them. First, their "love." Love for God and man is the essence of Christianity, the solvent of all wrongs, the fertile soil whence springs every virtue. When they put on love, they adorned themselves with a garment of exceptional beauty. (1 John 4: 20, 21; 5: 3; 1 Cor. 13: 1-13.) Second, their "faith." Faith ties man to his Maker. Faith reveals the great unseen world. Faith is developed by a study of the Bible. (Rom. 10: 17.) Third, their "ministry." From their love and faith flowed deeds of kindness. Love and faith in the heart find expression in life. (Gal. 5: 6; Heb. 6: 19.) Fourth, their "patience." They were constant and stedfast in their devotion. According to Thayer, patience is "the characteristic of a man who is unswerved from his deliberate purpose and his loyalty to faith and piety by even the greatest trials and suffering." (See James 1: 2-4; Heb. 10: 36.) And fifth, their progress. "Thy last works," said the Lord, "are more than the first." They had not become weary in well-doing. Their noble deeds had not diminished, but increased. They were unlike the saints in Ephesus, who had left their first love. Growth is the grand object of life, and where growth ends decay begins. (See 2 Pet. 3: 18.)

> "Not enjoyment, and not sorrow,
> Is our destined end or way;
> But to act, that each tomorrow
> Find us farther than today."

II. Condemnation (Verses 20-23)

20 **But I have this against thee.** The Son of God did not overlook the cluster of graces, he also saw their sins. **That thou sufferest the woman Jezebel, who calleth herself a prophetess; and she teacheth and seduceth my servants to commit fornication, and to eat things sacrificed to idols. 21 And I gave her time that she should repent; and she willeth not to repent of her fornication. 22 Behold, I cast her into a bed, and them that commit adultery with her into great tribulation, except they repent of her works. 23 And I will kill her children with death; and all the churches shall know that I am he that searcheth the reigns** (mind) **and hearts; and I will give unto each of you according to your works.** They demonstrated their love and faith by benevolent deeds, but lacked sufficient zeal and courage to maintain congregational discipline. Worldliness was in the church and tolerated there—"Thou sufferest," etc. Let us be reminded that we cannot please the Lord merely by letting evil alone: we must

actively oppose it. First, note the sinner tolerated, Jezebel. This name is symbolical. Likely, she was an outstanding woman who was to the congregation what Jezebel of Old Testament times was to Ahab and Israel—an unholy influence. (See 1 Kings 16: 31; 21: 25.) She was a self-styled prophetess—she "calleth herself a prophetess." Second, her sin. She refused to separate herself from idolatry; she also led others astray—"she teacheth and seduceth my servants," etc. It seems that the Balaamites, Nicolaitans, and the Jezebelites, with minor differences, were substantially the same—all were libertine sects, disclaiming obligation to moral law. They participated in the vilest fleshly sins and became the means of entangling others therein. And in her sin, Jezebel was obstinate: for "she willeth not to repent." She sinned against God's lovingkindness. (See 2 Pet. 3: 9.) Third, the punishment threatened. The leader and her followers were to share the "great tribulation." The "bed" mentioned was not a couch of revelry but of affliction. The place of pleasure was to become a place of pain. (See 2 Kings 9 and 10.) However, the punishment of her followers was conditional—"except they repent." Fourth, the purpose of the punishment. This was twofold: Retribution for sins, also an object lesson—"all the churches shall know," etc. (See Acts 5: 1-14; 1 Tim. 5: 20.) And fifth, Divine justice. "I will give unto each one of you according to your works." In these words, the impenitent can read his doom, and the penitent his salvation. (See 2 Cor. 5: 10; Rev. 22: 12.)

III. Encouragement (Verses 24-29)

24 But to you I say, to the rest that are in Thyatira, as many as have not this teaching, who know not the deep things of Satan, as they are wont to say; I cast upon you none other burden. "The deep things of Satan" likely means that those in error argued that it was to their advantage to learn the meaning of sin by actual participation in it; and that having experimental knowledge of it, they could indulge without injury to themselves. **25 Nevertheless that which ye have, hold fast till I come. 26 And he that overcometh, and he that keepeth my works unto the end, to him will I give authority over the nations: 27 and he shall rule them with a rod of iron, as the vessels of the potter are broken to shivers; as I also have received of my Father: 28 and I will give him the morning star. 29 He that hath an ear, let him hear what the Spirit saith to the churches.** As the trial was great, so was the encouragement. (See 2 Cor. 1: 7.) To those who had not yielded to the unholy influence, comforting words were spoken. Three promises were pledged. First, immunity, "I will cast upon you none other burden"—no other burden than that of setting themselves against the corruption around them. Many had conformed to the world, but a remnant was left— "the rest." They were admonished to "hold fast." Second, authority over the nations, or the evil powers that encircled them. The overcomer shall triumph over error and shatter the forces of immorality. Saintly men are powerful men, kingly men. They rule by a mighty weapon—wholesome influence. They subdue evil within and without. They reign with Christ, that is, in harmony with his will. And third, "the morning star." The dark cloud—the heathen element—shall disappear and the star of a dawning day shall shine. (See Rev. 22: 16.) And now comes the final and fitting admonition —the admonition to "hear what the Spirit saith to the churches."

From This Letter Learn:

1. That "the eyes of Jehovah are in every place, keeping watch upon the evil and the good." (Prov. 15: 3.)

2. That the Son of God discovers every virtue, also every vice. Known unto him is the deepest secret of the soul.

3. That the aim of the Christian is to "grow in the grace and knowledge" of the Savior. (2 Pet. 3: 18.)

4. That the "immoral life in one leader of the people is more pernicious than a whole street full of impurities in the lower quarters of the community, seeing that streams, foul and fair, cannot flow upward." (Landon.)

5. That it isn't enough for a Christian to refrain from immorality; he must also actively oppose it.

6. That if we become partakers of the sins of wicked leaders, we must also become partakers of their punishment. If we sin with them, we must also suffer with them.

7. That we learn "the deep things of Satan" by living in sin, but we learn to our shame and humiliation. When a child for the first time lays its hand on a hot stove, it learns a lesson—but it learns to its sorrow.

Memory Selection

"I know thy works, and thy love and faith and ministry and patience, and that thy last works are more than the first." (Verse 19.)

Daily Readings

Monday: The Baptism of Lydia. (Acts 16: 11-15.)
Tuesday: The Works of a Christian. (James 2: 14-26.)

Wednesday: "The Greatest of These." (1 Cor. 13: 1-13.)
Thursday: Faith and Its Triumph. (Heb. 11: 1-40.)
Friday: The Ministry of Love. (Matt. 25: 31-46.)
Saturday: "Put Away the Wicked." (1 Cor. 5: 1-13.)

For Class Discussion

1. Locate the city of Thyatira.
2. What can you say of this ancient city?
3. Relate the story of Lydia's conversion. What connection, if any, does her conversion have with the present lesson?
4. In verse 18, in what two figures does the Son of God present himself?
5. For what graces did he commend these Christians? What expression indicates their growth? How did they differ from the saints in Ephesus?
6. What did the Lord hold against them? Who was Jezebel of Old Testament times? in the church at Thyatira?
7. What threat did the Lord hold over the sinners in the congregation?
8. In verses 24 through 29 what encouragement do we find?
9. Discuss the practical points suggested in the lesson. Quote the memory selection.
10. Point out the relation of the daily readings with the lesson in hand.

LETTER TO THE CHURCH IN SARDIS

Text: Rev. 3: 1-6   Lesson VII

Traveling southward from Thyatira a distance of thirty-five miles, a messenger would arrive at Sardis, a very ancient city, the founding of which antedates known history. It was the capital of the kingdom of Lydia until the fall of Croesus in 546 B. C. Situated on almost inaccessible Mount Tmolus, which was strongly fortified, the city seemed impregnable. But Cyrus, seeing a man descend the precipitous rock by a secret passage, led his soldiers, one by one, up the steep ascent, to a place on the wall of the citadel which had been left unguarded, and took the city from wealthy Croesus. The fall of Sardis was due to overconfidence. Their strength became their weakness. Because they were not "watchful," the enemy came as a thief in the night. The citizens were aroused from lethargy, but too late.

The church at Ephesus, at Pergamum and at Thyatira received

praise mixed with blame; the church at Smyrna and at Philadelphia received praise and no blame; but Laodicea and Sardis received blame and no praise. As we open the six-verse letter, we note the following: The salutation; the church evaluated, the church admonished, a remnant praised, and promises to the victor.

Salutation (Verse 1a)

1a **And to the angel of the church in Sardis write: These things saith he that hath the seven Spirits of God,** that is, the fulness of the divine Spirit. (See John 3:34.) **And the seven stars,** or messengers. Having the Spirit in his perfect power and the messenger (ministers) of the word, the Lord was able to convict of sin, to reveal the hollow profession that prevailed, and to revive a dead congregation. As in each of the other letters, so in this one, the title assumed by the Son of God has special reference to the need and condition of the congregation. This will become more apparent as we advance.

I. The Church Evaluated (Verse 1b)

In this verse-portion we have two meaningful expressions setting forth two evaluations of the church. In the first, we have the evaluation of the sons of men, in the other the evaluation of the Son of God.

1. Of the Sons of Men

1b **I know thy works, that thou hast a name that thou livest.** Sardis was famed for spiritual vitality. Praise for her came from the lips of many. What were the things that probably gave her this fine reputation? A large membership, including people of prominence; financial power; an elaborate place of worship; an attractive ritual; soundness of doctrine; and cleanliness of morals. Ephesus had her Nicolaitans, Pergamum her Balaamites, and Thyatira her Jezebelites; but Sardis was free from false teachers and false doctrines. Those things which were so stoutly denounced in other congregations are not charged against the congregation in Sardis. We may therefore safely assume that they thanked God that they were not like other congregations. (See Luke 18:9-14.) Sardis was famed for her soundness! Soundness is essential, but soundness alone, like faith alone, is dead.

2. Of the Son of God

And thou art dead. Men said of Sardis, "She is alive." This was her reputation. The Lord said to her, "Thou art dead." This was her character. What men say of you is your reputation; what the Lord says of you is your character—what you really are. Imagine the feelings of those proud people, so accustomed to praise, when they heard this verdict one Lord's day! Activities were yet present—some works remained, though they were "ready to die." As in animals you may see muscular movements after life is gone, so Sardis was dead and all that could be seen were the ghastly twitchings of a corpse. As evidence of her lifeless state, no persecutions were leveled against this church. Why should Satan and his cohorts trouble themselves about a corpse?

II. The Church Admonished (Verses 2, 3)

2 **Be thou watchful.** How Christians need to heed this admonition! Be watchful over your affections. Allow them not to cling to an idol, nor to reach out after things forbidden. "Keep thy heart with all diligence." Be watchful against the devil: for he "walketh about, seeking whom he may devour." Be watchful against temptation: for it often comes from sources unexpected. **And establish the things that remain, which were ready to die.** This you can do by meditating upon the law of the Lord, by prayer, by assembling regularly with the saints, by engaging in public devotion, by lending a helping hand to a. brother in need. **For I have found no work of thine perfected before my God.** Their works had been weighed and found wanting. 3 **Remember therefore how thou hast received and didst hear.** Their memory was turned to the past for the sake of the present. They were of those "who, when they have heard the word, straightway received it with joy, and they have no root in themselves, but endure for a while. . . ." (Mark 4: 16, 17.) **And keep it**—the precious word—**and repent,** of present indifference. **If therefore thou shalt not watch, I will come as a thief, and thou shalt not know what hour I will come upon thee.** The city of Sardis had been captured twice because the sentries went to sleep on duty. Because Christians are careless, they become victims of the forces that war against them. "The Greek proverb, 'the feet of the avenging deities are shod with wool,' expresses the noiseless approach and nearness of Divine judgment, when they are supposed far off." (Trench.) "The last day is hidden from us, that every day may be observed by us." (Augustine.)

III. A Remnant Praised (Verse 4)

4 **But**—introducing a delightful relief—**thou hast a few names,** or persons, **in Sardis that did not defile their garments.** Sardis was dead, but a faithful few were left. They were known to the Lord. "He knoweth his own sheep by name, as he knew Moses by name,

and writeth the names of his own in heaven." (Bede.) They were "gleanings left in Israel" (Isa. 17:6), "the new wine found in the cluster" (Isa. 65: 8), the salt which saved the corpse from corruption. The wedding garment which they had put on in baptism was not defiled by sin. (See James 1: 27.) **And they shall walk with me in white; for they are worthy.** In this promise we see three things: Progress—"they shall walk"; partnership—"with me"; and purity— "in white." Noah walked with God; Enoch walked with God; so the remnant in Sardis walked with God. The atmosphere of the world is defiling. "But as the snow-white lily grows in the midst of the coal dust, so the Christian is able by God's grace to walk in the midst of a crooked and perverse generation and preserve in virgin purity his holy and spotless robes." The merit is not their own, but the Christ's, in whose precious blood their robes have been washed and by whose grace they are sustained. (1 John 1: 7.)

IV. Promises to the Victor (Verses 5, 6)

5 **He that overcometh shall thus be arrayed in white garments; and I will in no wise blot his name out of the book of life, and I will confess his name before my Father, and before his angels.** Though dead, Sardis was not hopelessly dead. It was possible, through divine power, for any member of the congregation to wrench himself from the death-grip. Unto the overcomer promises were made. First, a beautiful robe—"arrayed in white," the livery of heaven. White is a symbol of purity. (See Mark 9: 3; Matt. 28: 3; Rev. 1: 14; 2: 17; 6: 2; 20: 11.) Second, his name indelibly written in the book of life. In this book are inscribed the names of God's children. (See Luke 10: 20; Phil. 4: 3.) And now the overcomer is assured that his name shall be forever retained in the Father's family record. And third, his name confessed in heaven. During the days of his flesh, the Lord Jesus said, "Every one therefore who shall confess me before men, him will I also confess before my Father in heaven." (Matt. 10: 32.) "We may observe of this epistle that in great part it is woven together of sayings which the Lord had already uttered in the days during which he pitched his tent among men; he is now setting his seal from heaven upon his words uttered on earth." (Trench.) 6 **He that hath an ear, let him hear what the Spirit saith to the churches.** The words of the Spirit are the words of life. In these words there is life for all, even the **dead.** But all must hear and receive.

From This Letter Learn:

1 That the one who possesses the seven Spirits of God and the

ministers of the word has power to impart life, yea, to raise the dead.

2. That a man's reputation and his character are seldom the same. Reputation is the human evaluation—what men say of him; character is the Divine evaluation—what God knows him to be. A man's reputation may be good and his character bad; or his reputation bad and his character good.

3. That in all of our efforts we should strive to build character—a house that will stand the test when the rain descends and the flood comes and the winds blow and beat upon the house.

4. That whenever a Christian reaches the point in life where the world ceases to persecute him, we may safely conclude that he and the world have reached a compromise. Sardis was dead; for that reason she was free from persecution.

5. That a congregation may be doctrinally sound and morally clean, yet be lifeless. Was dead Sardis charged with false teaching or corrupt morals by the great Personality who knew all about her?

Memory Selection

"But thou hast a few names in Sardis that did not defile their garments: they shall walk with me in white; for they are worthy." (Verse 4.)

Daily Readings

Monday: "Dead While She Liveth." (1 Tim. 5: 1-25.)
Tuesday: "Having a Form of Godliness." (2 Tim. 3: 1-17.)
Wednesday: "In Works They Deny Him." (Tit. 1: 1-16.)
Thursday: "Awake Thou That Sleepest." (Eph. 5: 1-33.)
Friday: The Temptation of Jesus. (Matt. 4: 1-11.)
Saturday: The Lord Our Righteousness. (Rom. 10: 1-21.)

For Class Discussion

1. Locate the city of Sardis. (See map.) What can you say of this city? Tell the story of its capture.

2. Outline the letter to the church in Sardis.

3. In what words is Christ introduced to this church?

4. What can you say of the human evaluation of this congregation? How do you suppose the congregation gained a good name?

5. What can you say of the Divine evaluation? Was the congre-

gation sound in doctrine? in morals? Could she be sound in doctrine and morals, yet be dead? Discuss.

6. In verses 2 and 3, what admonitions are given? Discuss.

7. Were all the members of the church dead? What can you say concerning the faithful few?

8. What promises are given in verses 5 and 6? To whom were these promises given?

9. Quote the memory selection.

10. What practical points are suggested by the assignment?

11. Note the relation of the daily readings with the lesson text.

LETTER TO THE CHURCH IN PHILADELPHIA

Text: Rev. 3: 7-13 **Lesson VIII**

Philadelphia, a walled city of Lydia, was twenty-five miles southeast of Sardis, on the Cogamus River, a tributary of the Hermus. It was built by Atallus Philadelphus, king of Pergamos, a little more than a century before the birth of Christ. The fertility of the soil in this region has kept it peopled through the vicissitudes of the centuries. The city was destroyed by an earthquake in A.D. 17, but was soon rebuilt. Philadelphia, with ruins of ancient walls, is today a little city of some 10,000 souls. Its modern name is Allah Shehr, "city of God."

The meaning of Philadelphia is "brotherly love"; and the church in Philadelphia, like the church in Smyrna, received commendation and no censure. The Christians in this city were keepers of God's word; and, because they were keepers of the word, the Lord promised to keep them from coming trials and bless them with eternal rewards. The letter is a beautiful one and sets in motion thoughts most sublime.

Salutation (Verse 7)

7 **And to the angel of the church in Philadelphia write: These things saith he that is holy, he that is true, he that hath the key of David, he that openeth and none shall shut, and that shutteth and none openeth.** Contained in this verse is a three-point description of the Lord Jesus. First, he is "holy." In his moral nature, he is "without blemish and without spot." He "did no sin, neither was guile found in his mouth." Second, he is "true." He is not a false Messiah, but the true one—the fulfillment of Old Testament prophecy. And third, he "hath the keys," etc. This is the key to the door of opportunity, of advancement, of eternal security. Jesus has the sole power to admit or to exclude. (See Isa. 22: 20-22.)

I. Keepers of the Word (Verse 8)

8 **I know thy works.** Again we are reminded that Christ's judgment of his people is based on intimate knowledge. Knowing all about his people in Philadelphia, he was able to describe their lives and opportunities. **Behold, I have set before thee a door opened, which none can shut.** Paraphrase: "I have given thee an opportunity of which no man can deprive thee." This may mean one of three things. First, a door of evangelism, a special opportunity to preach Christ in places where he was unknown. Paul said, "A great door and effectual is opened unto me, and there are many adversaries." (1 Cor. 16: 9.) When he came to Troas for the gospel of Christ, "a door was opened unto" him "in the Lord." (2 Cor. 2: 12.) He urgently requested the brethren at Colossae to pray "for us also, that God may open unto us a door for the word, to speak the mystery of Christ." (Col. 4: 3.) Second, a door of refuge. That a trial of their faith was impending is indicated in verse 10. The Savior stood ready to admit the faithful into a door of refuge. And third, the door of eternal blessedness. This door is always open to God's people. (Read 2 Pet. 1: 10, 11.) **That thou hast a little power.** Her strength was little, but real; her influence in the community was small, but wholesome. Perhaps, this is why the Lord reminded them of the door opened; they needed this encouragement. Their very helplessness enlisted Omnipotence on their side. **And didst keep my word.** "Thy word have I laid up in my heart," said a psalmist, "that I might not sin against thee." By the process of study, we are to fill our hearts with the word; the word in the heart will keep us from sin and guide us in the performance of every worthy work. Satan endeavors to take away the word from the heart of the hearer. **And didst not deny my name.** This is another way of saying, "Thou has not been ashamed of my gospel." Though a local Jewish synagogue wielded a powerful influence against the Lord's people, they were steadfast in the faith. (Heb. 3: 14.)

II. The Keepers Are Kept (Verses 9, 10)

9 **Behold, I give** (or will make those) **of the synagogue of Satan, of them that say that they are Jews, and they are not, but do lie.** "The synagogue of Satan" refers to the Jews who depended on the fleshly relationship, denying that Christians, especially Gentile Christians, were the Lord's people. The only true Jews are those who accept the Christ. (See Rom. 2: 28, 29.) **Behold, I will make them to come and worship before thy feet, and to know that I have loved thee.** This triumph of the Christians, it seems, was to be brought about by the conversion of their foes. For a parallel, see Acts 16:

19-34. Paraphrase: "Not thou, by thy wealth or wisdom, but I, by my power, will bring about the triumph." The gospel of Christ, when preached in simplicity, will change a lion into a lamb. (See Rom. 1: 16.) 10 **Because thou didst keep the word of my patience, I also will keep thee from the hour of trial.** This has been called "the Divine lex talionsis," or law of retaliation. Forgive, and you shall be forgiven. (Matt. 6: 14.) "Judge not, and ye shall not be judged: and condemn not, and ye shall not be condemned: release and ye shall be released: give, and it shall be given unto you." (Luke 6: 37, 38.) Keep God's word, and you will be kept by God's power. **That hour which is to come upon the whole world, to try them that dwell upon the earth.** While sailing on the sea of life, we are baffled by waves of trials and temptations and tribulations; many go down to rise no more. But those who keep the word of God have the promise of being kept by the word. " 'The hour of trial' seems to be that which Christ had foretold should precede his coming, especially the triumph of anti-Christ. Hence the declaration in the next verse." (Pulpit Commentary.)

III. The Keepers Are Partakers (Verses 11-13)

13 **I come quickly,** to terminate your trials, to "receive you unto myself" (John 14: 1-3), to take vengeance on your foes (2 Thess. 1: 6-8). **Hold fast that which thou hast**—your strength, your zeal, your hope. Every virtue is a jewel most precious and should be retained at any price. **That no one take thy crown,** not for himself, but to rob you of it. Be patient, dear brethren. Hold what you have. Allow no temptation to entice you. In due time the storm will pass and deliverance will come. 12 **He that overcometh, I will make him a pillar in the temple of my God.** "The overcoming," says an eminent scholar, "is a continuous process, but will have a termination, and then he who has faithfully fought the daily battle will become a pillar." In the symbol of the "pillar" two ideas are embedded: Incorporation, for a pillar is a definite part of the temple; and permanence, for the pillar will stand as long as the temple stands. "The point is not 'he shall be one of the great and beautiful stones on which the others rest,' but 'he shall be so placed that he cannot be removed, while the whole fabric stands.'"—Cambridge Bible. **And he shall go out thence no more.** This is possibly an illusion to the people's fleeing from the city of Philadelphia because of the threat of earthquakes. The inhabitants of heaven shall be confronted with no threat. As long as he lives in the flesh, the Christian should watch and pray; he should take heed (1 Cor. 10: 12.) But the period of probation will soon be over, and he shall

be forever free from the possibility of falling away. The door which is opened for his deliverance will be closed for his security. "Who is there that would not yearn for the City, out of which no friend departs, and into which no enemy enters?" (Augustine.) **And I will write upon him the name of my God, and the name of the city of my God, the new Jerusalem, which cometh down out of heaven from my God, and mine own new name.** Note the threefold inscription. First, "the name of my God," because he is God's child; second, "the name of the city of my God," because he is an inhabitant of the holy habitation; and third, the Savior's "own new name," because he has been redeemed by the Savior's blood. (Rev. 19: 12.) "When Christ makes us completely his by writing his own name on us, he will admit us into his full glory, which is at present incomprehensible to us." (Plummer.) 13 **He that hath an ear, let him hear what the Spirit saith to the churches.** The man who will not receive the light, makes no correction, finds no encouragement.

From This Letter Learn:

1. That the meaning of Philadelphia is "brotherly love." Every church should be a church of brotherly love. (Heb. 13: 1.) Let it not be broken by the demon of malice.

2. That it is possible, under divine grace and guidance, for a congregation to attain a state of relative perfection. The Lord brought no charge against the church in Philadelphia.

3. That the Lord has set before you "a door opened"—an opportunity to evangelize, to advance the kingdom in your locality. Are your opportunities few, your resources next to nothing? Use what you have; they will be multiplied. Power unused becomes weakness.

4. That the word of the Lord is valuable beyond measure. Let us gladly receive it, eagerly treasure it, diligently keep it, lovingly share it.

5. That the keepers of God's word are kept by God's power. Do you believe in special providence? Yes. The keepers of the word and no one else is kept by Divine power.

6. That as long as we live in the flesh, there is a possibility of falling away; but once we are admitted into the city of God we shall be forever secure—there will be no danger of apostasy.

Memory Selection

"Because thou didst keep the word of my patience, I also will keep thee from the hour of trial, that hour which is come upon the whole world, to try them that dwell upon the earth." (Verse 10.)

Daily Readings

Monday: "The Seed is the Word." (Luke 8: 4-15.)
Tuesday: "They Then That Received His Word." (Acts 2: 1-41.)
Wednesday: "The Proof of Your Faith." (I Pet. 1: 1-12.)
Thursday: God's Abiding Word. (1 Pet. 1: 13-25.)
Friday: "Make Your Calling and Election Sure." (2 Pet. 1: 1-21.)
Saturday: The Holy City. (Rev. 21: 1-27.)

For Class Discussion

1. Locate Philadelphia. (See map.) What can you say concerning this city?

2. Draw a comparison between the church at Philadelphia and the church in Smyrna.

3. In verse 7, what three-point description is given of the Lord Jesus?

4. In verse 8, what is the meaning of "a door opened"? a "little power?" In the same verse, what commendation is given?

5. In verse 9, what is "the synagogue of Satan"?

6. What is the Divine law of retaliation in verse 10? What is "the hour of trial" in the same verse?

7. Explain: "I come quickly," in verse 11.

8. What promise is given to the overcomer? Discuss. What three-fold inscription shall the faithful receive?

9. What practical lessons do we gather from the assignment?

10. Quote the memory selection.

11. Give a class report on each of the daily readings.

LETTER TO THE CHURCH IN LAODICEA

Text: Rev. 3: 14-22   Lesson IX

Laodicea, a city of southern Phrygia, lay some sixty miles southeast of Philadelphia, but nearer Hierapolis and Colossea, with which it is associated by the apostle Paul. (Col. 4: 13-16.) Named at first Diospolis, then Rhoas, the city finally received the name of Laodicea from Antiochus II, who rebuilt it and beautified it, in honor of his wife Laodice, by whom he was later poisoned. To distinguish it from the other city by the same name, it was often called Laodicea on the Lycus. While never a city of much importance, it was, nevertheless, famous for its wealth, which arose largely from the excellence of its soft black wool, woven by the citizens into a fine fabric. Destroyed by an earthquake in A. D. 62, Laodicea was soon rebuilt by its wealthy citizens without state aid.

All that now remains of this ancient city is a village called Eski-hissar.

Concerning the founding of the Laodicean church, we have no direct information. It is not unlikely that the congregation was founded by Ephphras, of Colossea, through whom Paul probably learned of false teaching there (Col. 1: 7, 8; 2: 4, 8.), for the letter to the Colossians was also addressed to the Laodiceans (Col. 4: 16). It must have been near the close of the first century that the beloved John wrote the letter to the church in Laodicea, along with the entire book of Revelation. The importance of the congregation continued for some time; but its influence greatly waned, and the Turks pressed hard upon it. The warnings of the letter, if heeded at all, were eventually forgotten, and her candlestick was removed.

At Laodicea the circle is complete. The letter to Laodicea is the seventh and last in the series. Seven, we recall, is the number for entirety, completeness, perfection. The seven churches symbolize the church universal—the church of our Lord in every land and in every age of the world's history.

Of the seven churches in Asia, the church in Laodicea was in the saddest plight. The world was tolerated in Thyatira, yet she was blessed with a remnant; Sardis was dead, yet contained "a few names" with undefiled garments; but Laodicea was without even a remnant; concerning her no word of praise was spoken—all was blame and rebuke. Looking into the nine-verse letter we discover the luke-warmness of the Laodiceans, also the wisdom and warmth of the Lord.

Salutation (Verse 14)

14 And to the angel of the church in Laodicea write: These things saith the Amen (meaning, "so be it"), **the faithful and true witness, the beginning of the creation of God.** In the salutatory verse we have a three-point description of the author of the letter. First, he is "the Amen"—the word is here used as a proper name for the Christ, the only instance of such an application in the Bible. He is unchangeable in nature, the guarantee of every word he utters. Second, he is "the faithful and true witness." He is competent to testify; what he says is a matter of knowledge; he is altogether worthy of trust. And third, he is "the beginning of the creation of God"—not the first creature that God made (the Father and the Son are co-existent), but the originating cause of all creation, material and spiritual. (See Col. 1: 15-18.)

I. Lukewarmness (Verses 15, 16)

15 **I know thy works.** Because he loved them, he told them of their true condition and earnestly admonished them to make amends. **That thou art neither cold nor hot.** They were afflicted with a "condition of soul wretchedly fluctuating between a torpor and fervor of love." (Trench.) Lukewarmness is a negative attitude toward both good and evil. In the heart of the lukewarm Christian, good and evil meet and are neutralized. He has enough Christianity to lull the conscience to sleep, but not enough to save the soul. The cause of such a spiritual condition is diversity of interests. The heart of man, with all of its capacity, is not large enough to contain the Lord 'and the world at the same time. His love for the world will stifle his love for the Lord. (See 1 John 2: 15; 2 Tim. 2: 4; Luke 10: 28-42.) **I would thou wert cold or hot.** The Lord prefers either extremity to a state of lukewarmness. Even the alien sinner is preferred to the half-hearted Christian. This is true because such a Christian is under a delusion, which makes him more difficult to reach. The lukewarm soul is the breeding place for all manner of sin. (See Luke 8: 14.) **So because thou art lukewarm, and neither hot nor cold, I will spue thee out of my mouth.** The Lord is endowed with emotions not unlike the emotions or feelings that we, as human beings, experience. However, there is a difference: His emotions are altogether pure, also more intense. We read of his grief (Gen. 6: 6), of his jealousy (Ex. 20: 5), of his anger (Jer. 4: 8), of his joy (Luke 15: 1-10), of his love and compassion (1 John 4: 8; Matt. 18: 27; but in verse 16 there is ascribed to him an emotion not attributed to him elsewhere in the Bible—the emotion of disgust. He says to Laodicea, "I am utterly disgusted with you." It is customary to serve hot and cold drinks at meals, but not lukewarm drinks. Lukewarm drinks are nauseating. A physician gives the patient lukewarm water to cause him to vomit. So, the lukewarm Christian is nauseating to the Lord and, unless his heart is warmed, the Lord will reject him.

II. Wisdom (Verses 17, 18)

17 **Because thou sayest, I am rich, and have gotten riches, and have need of nothing.** The city of Laodicea, with its natural beauty and material wealth, was a self-satisfied city; the church within the city had imbibed the same spirit. Likely the members regarded their prosperity as a token of divine approval, or evidence of their spirituality. The church was self-sufficient, self-satisfied, self-confident. Each one was saying, "I have need of nothing." Was their judgment of themselves the correct one? **And knowest not**

that thou art the wretched one and miserable (pitiable) and poor and blind and naked. In their spiritual pride, these Christians were in need of divine pity; "poor" in treasures laid up in heaven; "blind" to the dangers before them—blind to their own blindness; "and naked" of the garments that should adorn God's children. A terrible self-deception! On the verge of eternal ruin, and knew it not! "The first and worst of all frauds is to cheat one's self. All sin is easy after that." 18 I counsel thee to buy of me gold refined by fire, that thou mayest become rich; and white garments, that thou mayest clothe thyself, and that the shame of thy nakedness be not made manifest; and eyesalve to anoint thine eyes, that thou mayest see. Their own wisdom had led them to the brink of eternal ruin; now the Lord says, "I counsel thee." Because they were poor and pitiable, they were badly in need of "gold refined by fire" or treasures in heaven. Because they were naked, they were in need of "white garments" of the regenerate soul—the righteousness of the Lord. Because they were blind, they had need of eyesalve (faith) to enlighten their spiritual vision—they needed to learn the truth about themselves.

III. Warmth (Verses 19-22)

19 As many as I love, I reprove and chasten: be zealous therefore, and repent. Not a person loved of the Father escapes chastisement; if he is not chastened, he is not a son. (Heb. 12: 5-7.) The object of divine chastisement is to convict of sin and turn to repentance. (See 2 Pet. 3: 9.) 20 Behold, I stand at the door and knock: if any man hear my voice and open the door, I will come in to him, and will sup with him, and he with me. These beautiful words reveal three things. First, that Christ was on the outside, driven there by the indifference of church members. Second, that he was lovingly and tenderly seeking admittance into their hearts. "He at whose door we ought to stand, for he is the Door (John 10: 7), who, as such, has bidden us to knock (Matt. 7: 7; Luke 11: 9), is content that the whole relation between him and us should be reversed, and instead of our standing at his door, condescends himself to stand at ours." (Trench.) And third, on the condition that the door is opened, he will enter and spread a heart-warming feast. The Sun of Righteousness, like the natural sun, is ready to enter when the door is open—to flood the soul with light and love. When lukewarmness exists between friend and friend, there is nothing that renews warmth like communion. 21 He that overcometh, I will give him to sit down with me in my throne, as I also overcame, and sat down with my Father in his throne. The conqueror will be

enthroned. What an incentive! The justice of the Lord threatened to reject them—verse 16; now his mercy promises to exalt them if they will overcome the inertia of indifference. **22 He that hath an ear, let him hear what the Spirit saith to the churches.** In the word of God is embedded the warmth of God. He who gladly receives the word will be warmed by the word. His heart will throb with newness of life.

From This Letter Learn:

1. That, unless a Christian is careful, he will imbibe the spirit of the community in which he lives. The citizens of Laodicea were conceited, self-satisfied. The Christians in the city became like them. (See Rom. 12: 2.)

2. That lukewarmness is a powerful expellent. It expels Christ from the heart of a Christian. Did it not drive the Lord out of the hearts of the Laodiceans? Do we not find him on the outside? It also expels the Christian from the mouth of Christ. Did he not threaten to spue the Laodiceans out of his mouth?

3. That virtues and noble deeds do not thrive in the life of the lukewarm. How many virtues and how many noble deeds did the Lord find in the lukewarm Laodiceans? Not one, no not one!

4. That the remedy for lukewarmness is the Christ—more of his word, more of his zeal, more of his love.

Memory Selection

"Behold, I stand at the door and knock: if any man will hear my voice and open the door, I will come into him, and will sup with him, and he with me." (Verse 20.)

Daily Readings

Monday: A Double-minded Man. (James 1: 1-27.)
Tuesday: Faith and Works. (James 2: 1-26.)
Wednesday: Wisdom from Above. (James 3: 1-18.)
Thursday: The Friendship of this World. (James 4: 1-17.)
Friday: "Come Now, Ye Rich." (James 5: 1-19.)
Saturday: Supply the Graces. (1 Pet. 1: 1-21.)

For Class Discussion

1. Locate the city of Laodicea. (Point out on map.) Relate briefly its ancient history.

2. Do we know when or by whom the church was founded in this city? What reference does the apostle Paul make to this church? What other letter was directed to this congregation?

3. Compare conditions in this church with conditions in the church at Thyatira, at Sardis.

4. In the salutatory verse, what three-point description is given of the Christ?

5. What can you say concerning the lukewarmness of this church? What was the cause of it? To what danger did this condition subject the church?

6. In verse 17, what did they say of themselves? What did the Lord say of them?

7. In verse 18, what counsel did the Lord give?

8. Using verses 19-22 as the basis, discuss the Lord's remedy for their lukewarmness.

9. What practical lessons are suggested by the assignment?

10. Quote the memory selection.

11. Show that we have a remedy for lukewarmness in our daily readings.

PART II
The Book with Seven Seals
(Rev. 4: 1-8: 1)

PREPARATORY VISION

Text: Rev. 4 and 5   **Lesson X**

We come now to chapters 4 and 5, introducing the vision of the book with seven seals, which begins to unfold in chapter 6. Before we are allowed to look upon the horrible disclosures therein—the storm through which the church was to pass—we are given a glimpse of heaven, assuring us that God is on the throne and, no matter what the outward fortunes of the church may be in coming years, she will be victorious in the end: for he that is with her is mightier than they that be with her foes. (See 2 Chron. 32: 7, 8.)

The two chapters fall into three parts. In the first part the center of attraction is a throne and its Occupant; in the second it is a Lamb with a book; in the third part we hear a song unto the Occupant of the throne and unto the Lamb.

I. The Throne and Its Occupant (4: 1-11)

1 **After these things I saw, and behold, a door opened in heaven.** It was a door of intercourse—through it John heard a voice; it was a door of observation—through it he got a glimpse of glory. (See Matt. 3: 16, 17; Acts 7: 55, 56.) **And the first voice that I heard, a voice as of a trumpet,** resonant and distinct, **speaking with me, one saying, Come up hither,** through the open door into the realm of the Spirit. A higher insight into things spiritual was to be given. **And I will show thee the things which must come to pass hereafter**— from the time that John wrote. He had been writing of "the things which are" (things then present); now, he is to write of things then future. 2 **Straightway I was in the Spirit,** a state of spiritual ecstacy; **and behold, there was a throne set in heaven, and one sitting upon the throne.** Concerning his sacred Name, John was reticent. Note the description. 3 **And he that sat was to look upon like a jasper stone**—a stone of sparkling whiteness, indicating holiness. (See Isa. 6: 1-15.) **And a sardis**—a stone fiery red, indicating justice. There is terror in God's wrath (Heb. 12: 29). **And there was a rainbow round about the throne, like an emerald** (green) **to look upon.** The bow reminds us of the shipwreck of the world by sin

and the calm that followed (Gen. 9). The soft, mild, restful color denotes mercy. Thus the qualities of HOLINESS, JUSTICE and MERCY meet and blend in the God of the universe. **4 And round about the throne were four and twenty thrones,** lower, of course, than the grand central throne. **And upon the thrones I saw four and twenty elders sitting.** The number reveals their identity—the twelve patriarchs of the Old Testament plus the twelve apostles of the New, representatives of God's universal church—the glorified church of both dispensations. **Arrayed in white garments,** indicating their purity, **and on their heads crowns of gold,** reminding us of their victory. **5 And out of the throne proceed lightnings and voices and thunders.** The setting is "symbolical of the power and majesty of God, as of old he manifested his presence on Sinai." (See Ex. 19.) **And there were seven lamps of fire burning before the throne, which are the seven Spirits of God**—"the Holy Spirit in his sevenfold working; in his enlightening and cheering, as well as his purifying and consuming energy." (Alford) **6 And before the throne, as it were a sea of glass** (glassy sea) **like unto crystal.** Reminding us of the brazen sea before the sanctuary in which the priests cleansed themselves before entering the temple service. (See 1 Kings 7.) A symbol of baptism. Both figures—lamps of fire and the glassy sea—remind us that unless we are born of water and the Spirit we cannot become "priests and kings unto God." (See John 3: 1-5.) **And in the midst of the throne, and round about the throne, four living creatures,** one for each of the four sides, **full of eyes before and behind.** They are servants, vigilant servants. They look every way. They observe everything. **7 And the first creature was like a lion, and the second creature like a calf, and the third creature had a face as of a man, and the fourth creature was like a flying eagle.** The "creatures" are attendants of the eternal throne. They are angels of a high order, perhaps the cherubim. (See Gen. 3: 24; Ex. 25: 21, 22; Ezek. 1 and 10.) **8 And the four living creatures, having each one of them six wings.** In Isa. 6: 2 each of the seraphim "had six wings; with twain he covered his face, and with twain he covered his feet, and with twain he did fly." These actions appear to indicate reverence, humility, and a readiness to obey. **Are full of eyes round about and within,** a symbol of watchfulness and perfection of sight, in every direction. **And they have no rest day and night, saying, holy, holy, holy is the Lord God, the Almighty, who was and who is and who is to come.** Thus, the worship is begun by the "four living creatures." Their praise is endless: for "they have no rest day and night." The ground of the praise is the holiness, the power, and the eternity of God. **9 And when the living** creatures shall give glory and honor and thanks to him that sitteth on the throne, to him that liveth for ever and ever, 10 the four and twenty elders (the redeemed church) shall fall down before him that sitteth on the throne, and shall worship him that liveth for ever and ever, and shall cast their crowns before the throne, saying, 11 Worthy art thou, our Lord and our God, to receive the glory and the honor and the power: for thou didst create all things, and because of thy will they were, and were created. The worship begun by the "four living creatures" is taken up by the redeemed church. The ground of the praise is God's creative power. They are thinking of the wonders of God's great world and the heavens which declare his glory. (See Psalm 19: 1-14; 148: 1-18.)

II. The Lamb with a Book (5: 1-12)

1 And I saw in the right hand of him that sat on the throne a book. It was, therefore, a sublime book. Written within and on the back—no more room for writing. It was a complete book, containing the whole revelation of God concerning the subject of which it treats. Close sealed with seven seals. An obscure, a mysterious book. 2 And I saw a strong angel proclaiming with a great voice, Who is worthy to open the book, and to loose the seals thereof? 3 And no one in the heaven, or on the earth, or under the earth, was able to open the book, or to look thereon. 4 And I wept much, because no one was found worthy to open the book, or to look thereon. From "a strong angel" came a ringing challenge. Though his mighty voice penetrated heaven, earth, and hades, "no one was found worthy to open the book." The aged seer "wept much" because revelation was apparently checked. 5 And one of the elders, a representative of the glorified church, saith unto me, Weep not: behold, the Lion that is of the tribe of Judah, the Root of David, hath overcome to open the book and the seven seals thereof. John was greatly comforted when the opener of the book was found. He was introduced to the seer by "one of the elders" as "the Lion," strong and stately, "of the tribe of Judah"; as "the Root of David," bearing marks or royalty; as the triumphant one, having gained a marvelous victory. 6 And I saw in the midst of the throne and of the four living creatures, and in the midst of the elders, a Lamb standing, as though it had been slain, having seven horns, and seven eyes, which are the seven Spirits of God, sent forth into all the earth. John had been told of a "Lion"; turning, he beheld "a Lamb." First, note the position he occupied: "In the midst," etc. He is the central figure. Both creation and redemption look to him. Second, the experience through which he had passed: He had "been slain."

On him the slaughter-marks were visible. (See John 1: 36; Isa. 53: 1-7.) Third, his attitude: He was "standing"—a triumphant attitude. No longer was he in the tomb, but living again. And fourth, the Lamb's ability: Omnipotent, "having seven horns"; and omniscient—"seven eyes," etc. He was eminently qualified, therefore, to open the book. **7 And he came, and he taketh it out of the right hand of him that sat on the throne. 8 And when he had taken the book, the four living creatures and the four and twenty elders fell down before the Lamb, having each one a harp,** a symbol of praise, **and golden bowls full of incense, which are the prayers of the saints. 9 And they sing a new song, saying, Worthy art thou to take the book, and to open the seals thereof: for thou wast slain, and didst purchase unto God with thy blood men of every tribe, and tongue, and people, and nation, 10 and madest them to be unto our God a kingdom and priests; and they reign upon the earth. 11 And I saw, and I heard a voice of many angels round about the throne and the living creatures and the elders; and the number of them was ten thousand times ten thousand, and thousands of thousands; 12 saying with a great voice, Worthy is the Lamb that hath been slain to receive the power, and riches, and wisdom, and might, and honor, and glory, and blessing.** Thus, the Lamb is accorded the right to break the seals, or to reveal the contents of the mysterious book. First, by the Eternal God. Into the hand of the Lamb, God entrusted the book. Jesus alone has the right to interpret the mind or purpose of the Father. Second, by the "living creatures." By their praise, they concede unto him the right. Third, by the glorified church. The praise and the prayers of the redeemed saints are heard. The theme is not creation, but redemption—"Redemption's Sweet Song." The "new song" is the song of the "new creation." And fourth, by an innumerable company of angels. They are not subjects of redemption, yet they are interested in the redemption of man. (Luke 15: 10.) So, they join the song of the saints in a responsive strain. Perfect praise ascends—seven things are ascribed unto the Lamb. Note them in verse 12.

III. Unto God, and Unto the Lamb (Verses 13, 14)

13 And every created thing which is in heaven, and on the earth, and under the earth, and on the sea, and all things that are in them, heard I saying, Unto him that sitteth on the throne, and unto the Lamb, be the blessing, and the honor, and the glory, and the dominion, for ever and ever. 14 And the four living creatures said, Amen. And the elders fell down and worshipped. The climax is reached when the voice of every created thing is lifted. Throughout the universe is heard a harmonious song. The "four living creatures" conclude the song with a mighty "Amen." The glorified church, now too full to speak, fell down in silent worship.

From These Chapters Learn:

1. That God is on the throne. This assures the ultimate triumph of his people.

2. That, of all the beings in the vast universe, Jesus alone is qualified to reveal or to unfold the plan and purpose of God. God has spoken unto us through his Son. (Heb. 1: 1, 2.)

3. That unto the Lamb that has been slain is due the sevenfold or perfect praise. He is altogether worthy "to receive the power, and riches, and wisdom, and might, and honor, and glory, and blessing."

Memory Selection

"Unto him that sitteth on the throne, and unto the Lamb, be the blessing, and the honor, and the glory, and the dominion, for ever and ever." (Chapter 5: 13b.)

Daily Readings

Monday: "Four Living Creatures." (Ezek. 1: 1-28; 10: 1-22.)
Tuesday: Song of the Seraphim. (Isa. 6: 1-8.)
Wednesday: The Majesty of God. (Ex. 19: 1-25.)
Thursday: "Behold, the Lamb of God." (John 1: 1-51.)
Friday: The Glory of God. (Psalm 19: 1-4.)
Saturday: "Praise Ye Jehovah." (Psalm 148: 1-14.)

For Class Discussion

1. Why should chapters 4 and 5 be studied together? Into how many parts do they fall?

2. Describe the eternal throne, as depicted in chapter 4.

3. Who are the twenty-four elders around the throne? What are the seven lamps and the glassy sea before the throne? Who are the "four living creatures" in the midst of the throne?

4. Describe the worship before the throne. Who were the participants? What was the theme of the song, creation or redemption?

5. Describe the book in the hand of the Throne-Occupant, as told in chapter 5.

6. From whom came a ringing challenge? What was the challenge? Why did John weep?

7. Who found a personality worthy to open the book? How was he introduced to John?

8. Show that Jesus is qualified to break the seals of the mysterious book.

9. Who accorded him the right to open the book? How?

10. In verses 13 and 14, unto whom was praise accorded.

11. What practical lessons are suggested?

12. Quote the memory selection.

THE OPENING OF THE FIRST SIX SEALS
Text: Rev. 6: 1-17   Lesson XI

We have finished a study of chapters 4 and 5, wherein the church was assured that God is over all, and that her future is committed to the Lamb. Now, in chapters 6, 7 and 8: 1, she is allowed to look into the future, with its trials and triumphs, as it is revealed by means of pictures. The study is most fascinating and we enter the divine picture-gallery with anxious expectations.

In the preceding chapter we learned that the Lamb had taken the sealed book from the hand of Him that sat on the throne. And now, in chapter 6 he opens the first six seals of the mystic book.

I. A White Horse (Verses 1, 2)

1 **And I saw when the Lamb opened one of the seven seals, and I heard one of the four living creatures saying as with a voice of thunder,** indicating the majesty of the speaker, **Come. 2 And I saw, and behold, a white horse, and he that sat thereon had a bow; and there was given unto him a crown: and he went forth conquering, and to conquer.** The word "come" was addressed by the lion-like creature (4: 7) to the mounted figure, and the response was immediate. This is a symbol, but what does it represent? First, it represents a war: for "he that sat thereon had a bow," an instrument of war. Second, a righteous war: for the horse was white, indicating truth and righteousness. The war is a bloodless one, led by the Captain of our Salvation. (Read 19: 11-16.) This war began when Jesus ascended to the right hand of God, a position of authority, and the disciples began to go everywhere at his command (Mark 16: 19, 20). Third, a triumphant war: for "there was given to him a crown," an emblem of triumph as well as loyalty. And fourth, an unceasing war: for "he came forth conquering, and to conquer." His victorious conquest knows no interruption. "He

must reign, till he hath put all of his enemies under his feet. The last enemy that shall be abolished is death" (1 Cor. 15: 25, 26).

II. A Red Horse (Verses 3, 4)

3' **And when he opened the second seal, I heard the second living creature saying, Come. 4 And another horse came forth, a red horse: and to him that sat thereon it was given to take peace from the earth, and that they should slay one another: and there was given unto him a great sword.** In response to the call of the calf-like creature, this figure came forth. Of what is it a representation? "'Probably it is enough to say that not one of the four riders is a person. Each is rather a cause, a manifestation of certain truths connected with the kingdom of Christ."—Milligan. First, this mounted figure represents a war: for "to him that sat thereon it was given to take peace from the earth." Second, a carnal war: for the horse was the color of blood, of fire, of violence. The earth was to be a slaughter house. In Matthew 24, Jesus says, "Ye shall hear of wars and rumors of wars" and "nations shall rise up against nation, and kingdom against kingdom." No particular war, but war in general is meant. Third, a war between the wicked: for "they"—the people of the earth—"slay one another." The murder is mutual—man murders man. The saints are slain, but they do not slay; they are often persecuted, but they do not persecute. And fourth, a mighty conflict, symbolized by "a great sword." Since the day the Lamb opened the seal to John on Patmos, millions have been slaughtered on fields of battle and rivers have flowed with human blood.

III. A Black Horse (Verses 5, 6)

5 **And when he opened the third seal, I heard the third living creature saying, Come, And I saw, and behold, a black horse; and he that sat thereon had a balance in his hand. 6 And I heard as it were a voice in the midst of the four living creatures saying, A measure of wheat for a shilling, and three measures of barley for a shilling; and the oil and the wine hurt thou not.** At the call of the man-like creature, came this grim figure. The color (black) is typical of distress, woe, mourning. The "balance" reveals the cause of the distress, namely, famine. It is during famine that food is doled out by weight (Lev. 26: 26; Ezek. 4: 16, 17), and only a small allowance can be purchased at the price of a day's earnings. During the extreme scarcity, "the oil and the wine" are sorely needed, so caution should be exercised concerning their use. A famine follows the sword, and Jesus had said, in Matthew 24, "there shall be famine in divers places."

IV. A Pale Horse (Verses 7, 8)

7 **And when he opened the fourth seal, I heard the voice of the fourth living creature saying, Come.** 8 **And I saw, and behold, a pale horse: and he that sat upon him, his name was Death; and Hades,** meaning, the dark region of the unseen world, **followed with him. And there was given them authority over the fourth part of the earth,** and no more: for the circle of their activity is limited. **To kill with sword, and with famine, and with death, and by the wild beasts of the earth.** At the call of the eagle-like creature, this mounted figure appeared. Pale or livid, a greenish hue, is the unmistakable token of the approach of death. The rider is Death— not death in some particular form, but Death itself. Following him, and ready to swallow up the slain, is Hades. Single forms of death —by war and famine—were revealed in the second and third seals; now the king of terrors himself appears, and in his cruel hand are gathered all forms of death—by war, by plague, by famine, by pestilence. There is a marked resemblance between this passage and Ezekiel 14: 21. How very dark and dreadful is the fourth seal!

V. Souls Under the Altar (Verses 9-11)

9 **And when he opened the fifth seal, I saw underneath the altar the souls of them that had been slain for the word of God, and for the testimony which they held:** 10 **and they cried with a great voice, saying, How long, O Master, the holy and true, dost thou not judge and avenge our blood on them that dwell on the earth?** 11 **And there was given them to each one a white robe; and it was said unto them, that they should rest yet for a little time, until their fellow-servants also and their brethren, who should be killed even as they were, should have fulfilled their course.** In these verses we are reminded that the death of martyrs, so common in John's day, is not unnoticed or unregarded by the Lord. Under the Old Covenant, victims were sacrificed on the brazen altar at the entrance of the tabernacle (Ex. 40: 29), and their blood was poured out at the foot of this altar (Lev. 4: 7). By yielding up their lives for the cause of righteousness, the martyrs are regarded as having offered themselves upon the heavenly altar. (See 2 Tim. 4: 6.) Like the blood of righteous Abel (Gen. 4), their blood ("souls" or "lives") is said to cry unto God for punishment. God heard the cry, but reminded them that final punishment for their persecutors must wait till the number of martyrs is fulfilled. Meanwhile the martyrs, now in the intermediate state, are given white robes, a symbol of their purity and a pledge of their glory.

VI. The Great Catastrophe (Verses 12-17)

As we read these verses let us remember that we are looking upon another picture. Though a picture, it represents something very real. In verses 12, 13 and 14 we have a mighty convulsion. In verses 15, 16 and 17 we have the fear and consternation that followed.

12 And I saw when he opened the sixth seal, and there was a great earthquake; and the sun became black as sackcloth of hair, and the whole moon became as blood; 13 and the stars of the heaven fell unto the earth, as a fig tree casteth her unripe figs when she is shaken of a great wind. 14 And the heaven was removed as a scroll when it is rolled up and every mountain and island were moved out of their places. "This description is marked by almost unparalleled magnificence and sublimity, and any attempt to dwell upon details could only injure the general effect. The real question to be answered is, To what does it apply? Is it a picture of the destruction of Jerusalem or of the final judgment? Or may it even represent every great calamity by which a sinful world is overtaken? In each of these senses, and in each of them with a certain degree of truth, has the passage been understood. Each is a part of the great thought it embraces."—Milligan. To the fall of Jerusalem, to every great crisis in the history of the world, and especially to the end of all, the language may be fittingly applied. **15 And the kings of the earth, and the princes, and the chief captains, and the rich, and the strong, and every bondman and freeman, hid themselves in the caves and in the rocks of the mountains; 16 and they say to the mountains and to the rocks, Fall on us, and hide us from the face of him that sitteth on the throne, and from the wrath of the Lamb: 17 for the great day of their wrath is come; and who is able to stand?** These verses depict the panic that followed, which is universal in scope. The unbelievers from the greatest to the least are involved and deeply concerned—seven classes are specified. By two things the panic is characterized: First, their shame—they attempt to conceal themselves; second, an acknowledgment of the approaching end and their unprepared state. But before the final stroke is delivered the elect must be gathered out (Matt. 24: 29-31); the saints must be made secure.

From This Chapter Learn:

1. That the book of Revelation is a book of pictures, of symbols. This means that we are to find the truth beyond the actual words.

2. That the white horse and its rider symbolize the cause of Christ, with which every Christian is identified.

3. That the red horse and its rider symbolize carnal war, by which the fortunes of the church are often affected.

4. That the black horse and its rider symbolize famine and its attendant evils.

5. That the pale horse and its rider represent Death, whose sway is universal.

6. That the souls under the altar represent the people who have suffered for righteousness' sake, even to the point of death.

7. That the great catastrophe represents the judgments of God against the ungodly of earth.

Memory Selection

"The great day of their wrath is come; and who is able to stand?" *(Verse 17.)*

Daily Readings

Monday: "Behold, a White Horse." (Rev. 19: 1-21.)
Tuesday: "He Must Reign." (1 Cor. 15: 1-26.)
Wednesday: War, Famine, Earthquake. (Matt. 24: 1-51.)
Thursday: Eating Bread by Weight. (Ezek. 4: 1-17.)
Friday: Sword, Famine, Evil Beasts, Pestilence. (Ezek. 14: 1-23.)
Saturday: Judgment of the Nations. (Matt. 25: 31-46.)

For Class Discussion

1. In chapters 4 and 5, what assurance do the saints find?

2. In chapters 6, 7 and 8: 1, what revelation is made to the church? By what means?

3. In chapter 6, what is the Lamb doing?

4. What is the content of the first seal? Of what is it a representation?

5. What is the content of the second seal? Give the meaning of it?

6. What was seen when the third seal was broken? Explain its significance.

7. When the fourth seal was broken, what did John see? What does it signify?

8. When the fifth seal was broken, what did John see? Who

were the souls under the altar? What did they cry? What answer was given?

9. What verses describe the great catastrophe? Give a word picture of the convulsion. Describe the reaction on the part of the ungodly.

10. What are the practical lessons suggested by the study?

11. Give a report on each of the daily Bible readings.

CONSOLATORY VISIONS
and
THE OPENING OF THE SEVENTH SEAL

Text: Rev. 7: 1-17; 8: 1   Lesson XII

When the last lesson closed, we were under a cloud. In the lesson we now enter, we have a rift in that cloud. Our text reminds us that triumph, not tribulation, is the last word in the history of the church. The church under the cross becomes the church crowned and triumphant. Though Christ's people pass through tribulation, they shall in due season enter into glory.

The violent disturbances disclosed with the opening of the sixth seal are on point of descending like a mighty storm upon the earth; but before it strikes, there comes a lull—a period of suspended judgment. "A whole chapter intervenes. Might it not be apprehended that amidst convulsions so terrific the church itself might founder? Who shall secure Christ's servants against being involved in that catastrophe?" God's servants must be sealed, their security assured. In the stillness before the storm, there came to John two consolatory visions which were meant to brace him and Christians of all generations for their trials: First, the sealing of the saints; second, a great multitude before the throne. After these visions, the seventh and last seal was opened.

I. God's Servants Sealed (7: 1-8)

1 **After this,** that is, the opening of the sixth seal, **I saw four angels standing at the four corners of the earth, holding the four winds of the earth, that no wind should blow on the earth, or on the sea, or upon any tree.** "Four" is a universal number, comprehending all directions—north, south, east and west. "Winds" denote calamities, perhaps the calamities revealed in the opening of the sixth seal, under another figure. (See Jer. 49: 36; Dan. 7: 2; Matt. 24: 31.) Thus, the angels were restraining universal calamities, holding them like dogs on a leash. The destructive agencies were

—53—

suspended for the preservation of God's elect. **2 And I saw another angle ascend from the sunrising,** the region whence the Savior himself, the dayspring from on high, the morning star, came on a mission of mercy, **having the seal of the living God: and he cried with a great voice to the four angels to whom it was given to hurt the earth and the sea, 3 saying, Hurt not the earth, neither the sea, nor the trees, till we shall have sealed the servants of our God on their foreheads.** Who is this angel from the sunrising? The great Angel of the Covenant fits well the description. "He came from the orient depth of glory with Divine credentials and with great earnestness, in order to stay the angels of retribution from executing their terrible commission. Our blessed Redeemer holds back the hand of the destroying angel." To the Lord Jesus we owe the delay of judgment. God's love is of such a nature that he cannot curse anything until his people are sealed or marked for security. (See Gen. 19: 22; Ex. 12: 7-13; Ezek. 9: 3-6; Matt. 24: 21.) **4 And I heard the number of them that were sealed, a hundred and forty and four thousand, sealed out of every tribe of the children of Israel:**

5 Of the tribe of Judah were sealed twelve thousand;
Of the tribe of Reuben twelve thousand;
Of the tribe of Gad twelve thousand;
6 Of the tribe of Asher twelve thousand;
Of the tribe of Naphtali twelve thousand;
Of the tribe of Manasseh twelve thousand;
7 Of the tribe of Simeon twelve thousand;
Of the tribe of Levi twelve thousand;
Of the tribe of Issachar twelve thousand;
8 Of the tribe of Zebulun twelve thousand;
Of the tribe of Joseph twelve thousand;
Of the tribe of Benjamin were sealed twelve thousand.

"A hundred and forty and four thousand" is a symbolic number, representing completeness. Twelve is a sacred number—the number of the church, or of God's people. It is multiplied by itself, then by one thousand, an exalted number. One hundred and forty and four thousand is the result. The number is not literal, but figurative—a number that stands for all the redeemed of all ages of the world. "Israel" is not here used in a fleshly sense, but in a spiritual—as Paul had used it (Rom. 9: 6; Gal. 3: 26-29; 6: 16), and as John himself later used it (Rev. 21: 12).

II. The Great Multitude (Verses 9-17)

Both visions refer to the same people, but under different aspects. In the first, they are only sealed, and through the sealing made secure. In the second they are more than secure—they have peace and joy, and every sorrow is healed.

9 **After these things I saw, and behold, a great multitude, which no man could number, out of every nation and of all tribes and peoples and tongues.** All the departed saints, and all the living saints, and all the saints who shall live, are included in the number. The vastness of the throne is disclosed in the four-part phrase, "out of every nation and of all tribes and people and tongues." From every continent and island of the sea they are gathered. **Standing before the throne,** a favorable position—a position of security and joy, **and before the Lamb,** by whom they had been redeemed. **Arrayed in white robes.** The "robe" is the character in which, as the result of his deeds and habits, a man drapes himself. "White" has always been heaven's color, indicating immaculate purity. **And palms in their hands.** "The palm-bearing multitude before the throne suggests to us the thought of rejoicing at ,the close of the harvest. A year's work is done, the sowing days are over, the reaping days are come. . . . And so the metaphor of my text opens out into that great thought that the present and the future are closely continuous, and that the latter is the time for realizing, in one's own experience, the results of the life that we live here. Today is the time of sowing; the multitude with the palms in their hands are reapers."—Maclaren. 10 **And they cry with a great voice, saying, Salvation unto our God who sitteth on the throne, and unto the Lamb.** 11 **And all the angels were standing about the throne, and about the elders,** four and twenty in number, **and the four living creatures,** a high order of angels, **and they fell before the throne on their faces, and worshipped God,** 12 **saying, Amen: Blessing, and glory, and wisdom, and thanksgiving, and honor, and power, and might, be unto our God for ever and ever. Amen.** In verse 12, beginning and ending with a grand "Amen," we have the seven-fold or perfect praise ascribed unto God the Father. The position of the angels is around the throne, while the elders, representing the glorified church, and the four living creatures form the inner circle. 13 **And one of the elders answered, saying unto me, These that are arrayed in the white robes, who are they, and whence came they?** 14 **And I say unto him, My Lord, thou knowest. And he said to me, These are they that come out of the great tribulation, and they washed their robes, and made them white in the blood of the Lamb.** They are not angels, but human beings who had known temptation, sin, sorrow, bereavement, the bitterness of persecution and the blessed gospel experience. Unto their souls had been applied the cleansing power of the Lamb. 15 **Therefore are they before the**

throne of God; and they serve him day and night in his temple.
Their service is continual, uninterrupted. **And he that sitteth on
the throne shall spread his tabernacle over them.** From trials and
persecutions and temptations they are shielded by Divine power.
**16 They shall hunger no more, neither thirst any more; neither shall
the sun strike upon them, nor any heat: 17 for the Lamb that is
in the midst of the throne shall be their shepherd, and shall guide
them unto fountains of water of life: and God shall wipe away
every tear from their eyes.** All their wants are supplied; they are
beyond reach of harm; and all sadness is taken away. There are
tears of pity—compassionate people weeping the fearful doom of
hardened sinners (Luke 19: 41, 42); there are tears of sympathy—
tenderhearted friends who share sorrows, who weep with the ones
who weep (John 11: 25); there are tears of bereavement—a David
weeping for his son Absalom (2 Sam. 18: 33), or a Rachel weeping
for her children because they are not (Matt. 2: 16-18); there are
tears of penitent souls who weep the memory of wasted lives (Luke
7: 36-38); there are tears of anxiety—earnest Christian workers who
are deeply concerned with the moral and spiritual well-being of
the people with whom they live and labor (Acts 20: 31); and there
are tears of sacrifice—tears of God's children who suffer great personal loss to the end that the church may go forward, that the
gospel may be preached in those places where it has never been
heard (Psalm 126: 5; Acts 20: 19). But God, with a tender hand,
"shall wipe away every tear from their eyes."

III. Silence in Heaven (8: 1)

**1 And when he opened the seventh seal, there followed a silence
in heaven about the space of half an hour.** When the sixth seal was
opened, there was a commotion (6: 12). When the seventh was
opened there was an awful silence—for a brief period, heaven
awaited in hushed awe. This silence is typical of the peace that
reigns in heaven, the ineffable joy beyond the comprehension of
mortal man. Such a scene prepared the aged seer and all the saints
for the judgment to come. "Silence is the element in which great
things fashion themselves together; that at length they may emerge
full-formed and majestic, into the delight of life which they are
henceforth to rule."—Thomas Carlyle.

From the Text We Learn:

1. That calamities of gigantic proportions are held like dogs on
the leash, ready to be loosed at the proper moment.

2. That before calamities descend, God provides for the se-

curity of his servants. In fact, he has already made ample provisions through the reign of his beloved Son.

3. That the future of the faithful Christian is more than secure: It is filled with peace and joy beyond the power of words to express. Even in the life that now is, the joy of a Christian far exceeds the sorrows he is called upon to bear or to share. He has nothing to fear this side of death; he has nothing to fear beyond death. No man can do him permanent injury.

Memory Selection

"The Lamb that is in the midst of the throne shall be their shepherd, and shall guide them unto fountains of waters of life: and God shall wipe away every tear from their eyes." (Verse 17.)

Daily Readings

Monday: "The Four Winds." (Jer. 49: 1-39.)
Tuesday: The Seal of Blood. (Ex. 12: 1-51.)
Wednesday: Jesus, Our Mediator. (Heb. 9: 1-28.)
Thursday: The Sheep and the Goats. (Matt. 25: 31-46.)
Friday: Looking Backward. (Rev. 6: 1-17.)
Saturday: Looking Forward. (Rev. 8: 2-13.)

For Class Discussion

1. Note the contrast between chapters 6 and 7.

2. Why the consolatory visions in chapter 7?

3. What is the significance of the number "four" in the book of Revelation? Of "winds?" Of the "four winds?"

4. Tell the mission of the angel of mercy in verses 3 and 4. Do you think this angel is the Lord Jesus or his representative? Why do you answer as you do?

5. What is the meaning of the sealing?

6. Who were the 144,000? Do you suppose the number is to be taken literally? Are they reckoned according to their racial or spiritual nature? Why do you answer as you do?

7. Give a word-picture of the great multitude in verses 9-17. Note that this vision is separate from the preceding vision.

8. Whence came they? Were they happy? Why do you answer as you do?

9. What followed the opening of the seventh and last seal? What does this signify?

10. What consolation may we, as Christians, draw from the assignment?

11. Quote the memory selections; also give a class-report on the daily readings.

PART III

The Seven Trumpets

(Rev. 8: 2-11: 19)

PREPARATORY VISION
and
THE FIRST FOUR TRUMPETS

Text: Rev. 8: 2-12   **Lesson XIII**

Passing from the vision of the seven seals, we come to the vision of the seven trumpets. Each of these visions is separate and distinct. The number seven, associated with the seven seals and also with the trumpets, indicates the complete nature of each vision. One does not follow the other in chronological order. Instead, the events depicted in the vision of the trumpets are synchronous or simultaneous with those symbolized by the seals.

During the seven days of destruction of the city of Jericho, a symbol of all that is wicked and worldly, trumpets were employed (Joshua 6). So, the trumpets in the Revelation are used in announcing the judgment of the world. The seven trumpet-blasts are divided into two groups of four and three. The first four deal more directly with the lower creation: for by them the land, the sea, the fountains and the atmosphere are affected. The last three deal more directly with men. Because they affect men with pain, death and hell, they are called the woe-trumpets.

Preparatory Vision (Verses 2-6)

2 And I saw the seven angels that stand before God; and there were given unto them seven trumpets. Who were these angels? They were angels of irresistible power—so indicated by their number; they were angels of prominence—so indicated by their position—they stand "before God;" and they were angels of war: for a trumpet was a war signal. A war of divine retribution was at hand.

3 And another angel came and stood over the altar, having a golden censer; and there was given unto him much insense, that he should add it unto the prayers of all the saints upon the golden altar which was before the throne. 4 And the smoke of the incense, with the prayers of the saints, went up before God out of the angel's hand. 5 And the angel taketh the censer; and he filleth it with the fire of the altar, and cast it upon the earth: and there followed

thunders, and voices, and lightnings, and an earthquake. Our attention is here arrested by the following. First, the appearance of "another angel," a ministering spirit (Heb. 1: 14) doing the bidding of God in the mighty drama. Second, "the altar" over which he stood. The golden altar of insense which stood before the veil (Ex. 30: 6), now stands before the throne of God, the veil having been removed. Third, the ascending smoke, representing the insense-perfumed prayers of the saints, as they prayed for a speedy end of the world. (See 6: 10.) Fourth, the descending fire, symbolizing God's fiery judgment about to fall upon the foes of the church, in answer to the prayers. And fifth, the awe-striking phenomena—thunders, voices, lightnings, and an earthquake—reminding us that the God of vengeance is at hand.

6 **And the seven angels that had the seven trumpets prepared themselves to sound.** And now, the narrative in verse 2 is taken up and continued. The intervening verses serve to indicate the immediate cause of the retribution about to fall.

Though men had been repeatedly warned, they persisted in sin. By their hardness and impenitent heart they had treasured up for themselves wrath, and now the season of wrath and revelation of the righteous God has come. (Rom. 2: 4, 5.) The saints of the Lord, whose garments are unspotted, are by the plagues untouched.

I. The First Trumpet: Hail, Fire and Blood (Verse 7)

7 **And the first sounded, and there followed hail and fire, mingled with blood, and they were cast upon the earth: and the third part of the earth was burnt up, and all green grass was burnt up.** Against the ungodly, the forces of nature are turned. The land, the source of natural life, is smitten. Material things, when wisely used, become a blessing; when abused a curse. "The third part" undoubtedly represents "a large part, but such that the greater part was still uninjured," indicating that mercy is still greater than judgment. In this retributive act, the seventh Egyptian plague is magnified—"blood" is added (Ex. 9: 23-25). If it seems difficult to grasp the full significance of every inspired expression, remember that one thing is crystal clear, namely, that men are punished by their sins and because of their sins, even while in the flesh. Sin and suffering are inseparable. In the experience of men, they are closely associated. "These punishments are not merely direct inflictions of plagues, but consist in great part of that judicial retribution on them that know not God, which arise from their own depravity, and in which their own sins are made to punish themselves."—Alford.

II. The Second Trumpet: The Burning Mountain
(Verses 8, 9)

8 **And the second angel sounded, and as it were a great mountain burning with fire was cast into the sea: and the third part of the sea became blood; 9 and there died the third part of the creatures which were in the sea, even they that had life; and the third part of the ships was destroyed.** Was it a volcanic eruption that John saw? After the first trumpet-blast, the land was affected; after the second, it was the sea. We are reminded of the first Egyptian plague (Ex. 7: 20, 21). Though the devastation was terrible, it was limited in scope: for only "the third part of the sea became blood" and "third part of the creatures" and of the ships therein were destroyed. The judgments, as they come in order, seem to increase in severity. The first trumpet-blast "affects vegetation, thus causing trouble, but not destruction to men; the second begins to affect animal life; the third causes many men to die; and the following one affect men with direct punishment." When the sons of men, in face of warning, continue in sins, their sorrows tend to increase. The vision of the burning mountain does not typify any great upheaval in particular, but all great upheavals or commotions in general. Let it be remembered that "the sea, as well as the productions of the earth, can be used by God as his agents to punish and warn mankind."

III. The Third Trumpet: The Blazing Star (Verses 10, 11)

10 **And the third angel sounded, and there fell from heaven a great star, burning as a torch,** that is, "with a flaring trail of fire." The falling of the stars in Matt. 24: 29 is a part of the general picture of the approach of the last judgment. We may conclude, therefore, that the burning star of this vision symbolizes an act of judgment sent upon an impenitent world. **And it fell upon the third part of the rivers, and upon the fountains of the waters.** The fountains—places where men drink—are poisoned. (Ex. 15: 23, 24.) Judgments are drawing nearer and nearer the ungodly. 11 **And the name of the star is called Wormwood,** a woody herb known for its bitter taste. The name points out the effect of the star, namely, bitterness of soul. (Lam. 3: 19; Jer. 9: 15.) **And the third part of the waters became wormwood, and many men died of the waters, because they were made bitter.** "It is hardly possible to read of this third plague, and not think of the deadly effect of those strong spiritous drinks, which are, in fact, water turned into poison."— Alford. It becomes increasingly clear that the events here depicted "carried one step further the description of God's vengeance on the

wicked, which has been already partially set forth." The star, the means here employed, "is typical of the awe-striking nature of the punishment, and is indicative of the fact that judgment is an act of God, and proceeds directly from heaven, and is not to be attributed to merely natural circumstances." After the first trumpet-blast, the curse fell upon inanimate nature; after the second, creatures with life suffered; after the third, human life was touched and taken— "many men died."

IV. The Fourth Trumpet: The Darkness (Verse 12)

12 **And the fourth angel sounded, and the third part of the sun was smitten, and the third part of the moon, and the third part of the stars; that the third part of them should be darkened, and the day should not shine for the third part of it and the night in like manner.** This takes us back to the ninth Egyptian plague (Ex. 10: 21-23). Not a third part of the unusual amount of light during the whole day and night is meant, but a total darkness one third of the day and the night. The Almighty God is able to turn the influence of the beneficient sun and planets into means of the destruction of the wicked. Remember, dear reader, that sin is followed by darkness—darkness within and darkness without. When Judas departed from the Lord, he went out into the darkness of the night (John 13: 30). All who depart from the Lord must face the darkness.

From These Verses Learn:

1. That, in answer to the prayers of his people, the Lord will send judgment upon the ungodly.

2. That the sons of men are punished by their sins and because of their sins.

3. That the anticipation of sin gives pleasure; the memory of it gives pain.

4. That the things of this life, when used wisely, become a blessing; when used unwisely they become a curse.

Memory Selection

"Be not deceived; God is not mocked: for whatsoever a man soweth, that shall he also reap." (Gal. 6: 7.)

Daily Readings

Monday: The Plague of Blood. (Ex. 7: 20-24.)
Tuesday: The Plague of Frogs; of Lice; of Flies. (Ex. 8: 1-32.)
Wednesday: The Plague of Murrain; of Boils; of Hail. (Ex. 9: 1-35.)
Thursday: The Plague of Locusts; of Darkness. (Ex. 10: 1-29.)
Friday: The First-born of Egypt Slain. (Ex. 11: 1-10; 12: 1-51.)
Saturday: Bitter Waters Made Sweet. (Ex. 15: 1-27.)

For Class Discussion

1. What can you say of the relation between the seven seals and the seven trumpets?

2. For what announcement were the seven trumpets used? Into how many groups are the seven trumpet-blasts divided? With what does the first group deal? The second?

3. What verses form the basis of our lesson? Into how many parts are these verses divided? What is the subject of each part?

4. Describe the preparatory vision, as given in verses 2-6. What is the main thought here?

5. What classes of people are affected by the seven trumpet-blasts? Are the people of God unhurt by these blasts?

6. Describe the first trumpet blast and the things that followed.

7. Describe the second trumpet blast and the things that followed.

8. Describe the third trumpet blast and the things that followed.

9. Describe the fourth trumpet blast and the things that followed.

10. What are some practical lessons taught or suggested by these trumpet blasts? Point out the connection between impenitence and these trumpet blasts.

11. Quote the memory selection.

12. Give a class report on the daily readings.

THE FIFTH AND SIXTH TRUMPETS

Text: Rev. 8: 13; 9: 1-21   **Lesson XIV**

We have just finished a study of the first four trumpet blasts, which set in motion forces of destruction that primarily affected objects of nature—the land, the sea, the fountains, the atmosphere. After an ominous introduction of the flying eagle, we pass on to the last three.

I. The Flying Eagle (8: 13)

13 **And I saw, and I heard an eagle,** a symbol of pillage and plunder, characterized by swiftness and strength. (Job 9: 26.) **Flying in mid-heaven**—not midway between earth and heaven but in direct line of the sun, a most conspicuous place where it could be seen

and heard by the inhabitants of earth. **Saying with a great voice, Woe, woe, woe, for them that dwell on the earth,** the ungodly portion of mankind, **by reason of the other voices of the trumpet of the three angels, who are to sound.** Because they seem to introduce woeful and wonderful things in the spiritual realm, they are called "woe trumpets."

II. The Fifth Trumpet: The Locusts (9: 1-12)

1 **And the fifth angel sounded, and I saw a star from heaven fallen unto the earth: and there was given to him the key of the pit of the abyss.** The star is an angel, not in the act of falling when John saw him—he had already fallen. He is the contrast and counterpart of him who is "the bright and morning star" and who holds "the key of death and hades." The fallen star must be Satan himself. (Isa. 14: 12.) "The pit of the abyss," over which he presides, is the lowest depth of depravity, the cavity whence comes evil, the abode of the devil and his angels (Rev. 20: 1-3; Luke 8: 31), not the lake of fire into which they will be eventually cast. (Rev. 20: 10.) 2 **And he opened the pit of the abyss; and there went up a smoke out of the pit, as the smoke of a great furnace; and the sun and the air were darkened by reason of the smoke of the pit.** 3 **And out of the smoke came forth locusts upon the earth; and power was given them, as the scorpions of the earth have power.** 4 **And it was said unto them that they should not hurt the grass of the earth, neither any green thing, neither any tree, but only such men as have not the seal of God on their foreheads.** The ascending smoke soon resolved itself into a swarm (cloud) of locusts. The locusts were not real—they did not thrive on vegetation. They are symbols of wild ideas and false doctrines, which becloud man's mental faculties. They have power to hurt or to disturb or to torment "only such men as have not the seal of God on their foreheads"—the unbelieving portion of mankind. God's people, who bear the seal of God, do not accept wild ideas or false doctrines; therefore they are by the power of evil undisturbed. 5 **And it was given them that they should not kill them, but that they should be tormented five months.** The mission of the locusts was to unsettle the minds of men, to inflict living misery. "Five months" perhaps means that the period of their work is limited. This was the period of time that natural locusts worked—from May to September. (Ex. 10: 12-14; Joel 2: 1-11.) **And their torment was as the torment of a scorpion, when it striketh a man.** When a person is stung by a scorpion, the spot immediately begins to inflame, becomes hard and red, and is affected with excruciating pain. Sin has power to torture the sinner. 6 **And in**

those days men shall seek death, and shall in no wise find it; and they shall desire to die, and death fleeth from them. "Death is universally regarded as the greatest evil, but such is the state of misery here that it is sought as a relief. How often is the life of a man rendered intolerable because of his sins, and he has recourse to a razor, the rope, the river, or the poison!"—Thomas. 7 **And the shapes of the locusts were like horses prepared for war.** In these words the general description of the locusts is given. **And upon their heads as it were crowns like unto gold, and their faces were as men's faces.** 8 **And they had hair as the hair of women and their teeth were as the teeth of lions.** 9 **And they had breastplates, as it were breastplates of iron; and the sound of their wings was as the sound of chariots, of many horses rushing to war.** 10 **And they have tails like unto scorpions, and stings; and in their tails is their power to hurt men five months.** In these words we have their specific description, in which seven characteristics are mentioned. Their power to torment is complete. Perhaps, no special significance should be attached to these details, which probably are only intended to increase the vivid horror of their picture. 11 **They have over them as king the angel of the abyss,** to whom we were introduced in verse 1: **his name in Hebrew is Abaddon** (destruction), **and in the Greek tongue he hath the name Apollyon** (destroyer). In the name we have the summation of the character of him who wears it. Satan is the destroyer of man—his character, his hope, his very life. (See John 8: 44.)

12 **The first Woe is past: Behold, there come yet two woes hereafter.** This is no more than a parenthetical remark of the seer between the fifth and sixth trumpet-blasts.

III. The Sixth Trumpet: The Armies (Verses 13-19)

13 **And the sixth angel sounded, and I heard a voice from the horns of the golden altar which is before God,** 14 **one saying to the sixth angel that had the trumpet, Loose the four angels that are bound at the great river Euphrates.** This is a voice of prayer. Observe, first, whence it came: "The (four) horns of the golden altar." This is the universal prayer of the saints. (See Rev. 6: 10; 8: 3.) Second, the request it conveyed: "Loose the four angels," etc. The chain-bound angels represent a destructive force which, until this moment, has been restrained. The river was Israel's natural boundary and defense on the northeast (Gen. 15: 18; 1 Kings 4: 21), symbolizing the longsuffering of God (2 Pet. 3: 9). Her foes—strong and ambitious—were waiting beyond. 15 **And the four angels were loosed, that had been prepared for the hour and day and month and**

year that they should kill the third part of men—a large part, though not the larger. 16 **And the number of the armies of the horsemen was twice ten thousand times ten thousand: I heard the number of them.** 17 **And thus I saw the horses in the vision, and them that sat on them, having breastplates as of fire** (red) **and of hyacinth** (blue) **and of brimstone** (yellow): **and the heads of the horses are as the heads of lions; and out of their mouths proceedeth fire and smoke and brimstone.** 18 **By these three plagues was the third part of men killed, by the fire and the smoke and the brimstone, which proceedeth out of their mouth.** 19 **For the power of the horses is in their mouth, and in their tails: for their tails are like unto serpents, and have heads; and with them they hurt.** In response to the prayers of God's people, symbolized by the voice from the altar, a destructive force was loosed at the appointed time. This is strikingly represented under the figure of the Assyrian cavalry. (See Hab. 1: 5-10.) To an Israelite the horse, often used in war, was an object of terror. First, note their number: two hundred million, representing a force irresistible. Second, their description. Their defensive strength is indicated in the "breastplates." Their offensive strength is indicated by their mouth whence emanate "fire and smoke and brimstone," and tails like unto serpents. And third, the havoc they work. The locusts could hurt only with their tails—horses with both tails and heads; the locusts could only sting—the horses can take life. As with the locusts, probably the detailed description of the horses has no special significance. The essential lesson is that when men persist in sin, evil consequences of irresistible proportions will follow. False doctrines and evil deeds bring upon the heads of the people who love them a power that bites and stings and crushes.

IV. Impenitence (Verses 20, 21)

20 **And the rest of mankind, the two thirds, who were not killed with these plagues, repented not of the works of their hands, that they should not worship demons, and the idols of gold, and of silver, and of brass, and of stone, and of wood; which can neither see, nor hear, nor walk.** In this verse, man's sins against God are mentioned; in the next, man's sins against man are mentioned. 21 **And they repented not of their murderers, nor of their sorceries, nor of their fornication, nor of their thefts.** All of these sins are in the plural except one—the sin of fornication. "Other crimes are perpetuated by men at intervals; there is one continual fornication within those who are wanting in purity of heart."—Bengel. When calamities came, like Pharaoh, they hardened their hearts. They were men set in their ways, clinging to false religion and sensualities. Their

afflictions, which increase in intensity, will reach the ultimate at the judgment of the last day.

From This Chapter Learn:

1. That the judgments of God affect not only the body, but also the mind of man. Sin is followed by painful mental reaction.

2. That the heart of the depraved is a cavity, whence issues all forms of evil: "for out of the heart come forth evil thoughts, murderers, adulteries, fornications, thefts, false witness, railing: these are the things that defile the man."—Jesus.

3. That the locusts of our lesson are of an order most terrible— "malicious as scorpions, ruling as kings, intelligent as man, wily as woman, bold and fierce as lions, resistless as those clad in iron armour."

4. That the impenitent man is powerless to resist the powerful and painful reactions to his own ungodly manner of life. "The way of a transgressor is hard."

5. That, in spite of self-inflicted sorrow, some men continue in sin. They are determined in their course. For them is reserved the lake of fire.

Memory Selection

"In those days men shall seek death, and shall in no wise find it; and they shall desire to die, and death fleeth from them." *(Verse 6.)*

Daily Readings

Monday: Looking Backward—The First Four Trumpets. (Rev. 8: 1-12)

Tuesday: Looking Forward—The Angel and the Little Book. (Rev. 10: 1-11)

Wednesday: A Devastation of the Land by Locusts. (Joel 1: 1-20)

Thursday: "As the Appearance of Horses." (Joel 2: 1-32)

Friday: "They Defile the Man." (Matt. 15: 1-39)

Saturday: "Sin, When It Is' Fullgrown." (James 1: 1-27)

For Class Discussion

1. Note the connection between this lesson and the preceding one.

2. At the sounding of the first four trumpets, what forces were set in motion?

3. With what striking vision is the last three woes introduced? Why are they called "woe trumpets"? With the sounding of these trumpets, what part of man is directly affected?

4. Describe the locusts that came after the sounding of the fifth trumpet. Whence did they come? Who opened the cavity for them? Who do they represent? What power do they possess? Who is tormented by them?

5. Tell of the sounding of the sixth trumpet and the things that followed. In verse 13, what is the "voice" from the horns of the altar? What petition did the voice convey? Describe the response. What does the mighty army represent? What is the essential lesson taught?

6. Did these calamities cause men to repent? In verse 20, what sins are specified? In verse 21, what sins are specified?

7. What lessons do we learn from the lesson?

8. Quote the memory verse.

9. Give a report on the daily readings.

INTERMEDIATE VISIONS—I
THE ANGEL WITH THE LITTLE BOOK

Text: Rev. 10: 1-11   **Lesson XV**

As between the opening of the sixth and seventh seals (7: 1-17), so between the sounding of the sixth and seventh trumpets, there is a pause or an interval during which two intermediate visions appear. The first is found in chapter ten, the second in 11: 1-13. We shall take a view of these visions, then pass on to the sounding of the seventh and last trumpet (11: 14-19).

Chapter ten, like other portions of the book, defy our ability to analyze. However, three divisions are reasonably clear. In the first we have the angel and the book; in the second, the angel's oath; and in the third, the book devoured.

I. The Angel and the Book (Verses 1-4)

1. **And I saw another strong angel**—able to carry into execution the task assigned. This is not the first "strong angel" that John had seen. (See 5: 2.) **Coming down out of heaven,** indicating his celestial origin and the importance of his mission. **Arrayed with a cloud,** a symbol of the glory of the Lord. (See 1: 7.) **And the rainbow was upon his head,** a token of the covenant of mercy. (See 4: 3; Gen. 9: 13.) **And his face was as the sun,** bright and glorious, **and his feet as pillars of fire,** consuming the ungodly as he advances.

2 **And he had in his hand a little book open.** Only two characteristics of the book are given. First, it is "little," in comparison with the book of seven seals. (See 5: 1.) Its contents do not directly concern so many people. Second, it is "open," not sealed as the former book, indicating that its decrees are to be forthwith executed. **And he set his right foot upon the sea, and his left upon the earth.** What a colossal figure! His position suggests two things: First, that the words he was about to utter were for the whole world; second, that he claims both land and sea for the Creator—both are about to be purged of the usurper and his followers. 3 **And he cried with a great voice, as a lion roareth**—loud, distinct, terrible. The voice was universally heard, like the voice of the other "strong angel" (5: 2). Was this the voice of the "Lion of the tribe of Judah?" The angel was either Christ or his representative. (Comp: 1: 14-16.) "Probably the whole incident is intended merely to set forth the powerful and terrible nature of the messenger who is to deliver God's message." **And when he cried, the seven thunders uttered their voices.** This was thunder in all of its varied terrors, a token of coming judgment. In addition to the judgments already foretold, there are others more terrible in the background. We recall that thunder, voices, lightnings and an earthquake preceded the trumpet blasts (8: 5). 4 **And when the seven thunders uttered their voices, I was about to write: and I heard a voice from heaven saying, Seal up the things which the seven thunders uttered, and write them not.** Their message was one of horror. Lest the saints be given to morbid ponderings and sinners driven to a life of reckless despair, John was forbidden to record what he had heard.

II. The Angel's Oath (Verses 5-7)

5 **And the angel that I saw standing upon the sea, and upon the earth lifted up his right hand to heaven,** in solemn gesture. Such action was customary among the Jews in swearing. (See Gen. 14: 22; Deut. 32: 40.) In Dan. 12: 7, both hands are uplifted, here only his right hand: for in the other was the book. 6 **And sware by him that liveth forever and ever, who created the heaven and the things that are therein, and the earth and the things that are therein, and the sea and the things that are therein.** By the Eternal One, by the Creator of all things the mighty angel swore. The decree, therefore, was irrevocable. **That there shall be delay** (time) **no longer.** "The great mystery of Time, were there no other; the illimitable, silent, never-resting thing called Time, rolling, rushing on, swift, silent, like an all-embracing ocean-tide, on which we and all the universe swim like exhalations, like apparitions which are and then

are not. This is forever very literally a miracle,—a thing to strike us dumb; for we have no word to speak about it."—Carlyle. **7 But in the days of the voice of the seventh angel, when he is about to sound, then is finished the mystery of God, according to the good tidings which he declared to his servants the prophets.** The martyrs had been crying, "How long?" They were told to "rest a little time" (6: 10, 11). Now, they are to rest no longer. In the days of the seventh trumpet-blast, the last judgment will fall, the end will come, the mystery of God will be finished. And amid the "wreck of matter and the crash of worlds," the mighty convulsions that shall shake the earth, we shall most assuredly want a Friend, a Rock of Refuge. There is One—and only One—who has the power to preserve us. That one is the Lord Jesus Christ. (Heb. 7: 25.) In him is rest and eternal security.

> "Then let the earth's old pillars shake,
> And all the wheels of nature break;
> Our steady souls should fear no more
> Than solid rocks when billows roar!"

III. The Book Devoured (Verses 8-11)

8 And the voice which I heard from heaven, mentioned in verse 4, **I heard it again speaking with me, and saying, Go, take the book which is open in the hand of the angel that standeth upon the sea and upon the earth.** "The charm of this symbolism is that it is so luminous that he who readeth may run." God's revealed will or plan is entrusted first to the "strong angel," and then by him to the beloved apostle. The same process of transmission is given in 1: 1-3. The Lord Jesus is the supreme Revealer. By him all the angelic hosts are commissioned. They are the immediate instruments through whom the word of God was given to the apostles. Under the new dispensation, as under the old, holy men of God spoke as they were moved by the Holy Spirit. **9 And I went unto the angel, saying unto him that he should give me the little book. And he saith unto me, Take it, and eat it up; and it shall make thy belly bitter, but in thy mouth it shall be sweet as honey.** A similar vision came to a prophet of the exile by the river Chebar. "And when I looked," he said, "behold, a hand was put forth unto me; and, lo; a roll of a book was therein; and he spread it before me: and it was written within and without; and there were written therein lamentations, and mourning, and woe. And he said unto me, Son of man, eat that which thou findest; eat this roll, and go, speak unto the house of Israel. So I opened my mouth, and he caused me to eat the roll. And he said unto me, Son of man, cause thy belly to eat, and fill thy bowels with this roll that I gave thee. Then did I eat it; and it was in my mouth as honey for sweetness. And he said unto me, Son of man, go, get thee unto the house of Israel, and speak with my words unto them." (Ezek. 2: 9-3: 4.) In like manner, the beloved John was to receive the book from an angel's hand, to digest it, to thoroughly master it, to the end that he might faithfully proclaim it to the people for whom it was intended. 10 **And I took the little book out of the angel's hand, and ate it up.** He studied it. He assimilated it. He made it a part of his mental-self. **And it was in my mouth sweet as honey: and when I had eaten it, my belly was made bitter·** The angel, knowing the contents of the book, mentioned the bitterness first; but the writer narrates his experience in historical or chronological order. The book was both sweet and bitter. At first John was delighted, because of the rare privilege granted—the privilege of receiving a message from heaven; but when he saw the future the book revealed—the "lamentations, and mourning, and woe"—he was deeply grieved. Honey in the mouth became bile in the stomach. 11 **And they say unto me, Thou must prophesy again over many peoples and nations and tongues and kings.** The word "prophesy" means to declare God's righteous acts and judgments. What John had learned from "the little book," he was to declare, to teach. This responsibility was laid upon him by a Divine command. He had already, in the early part of the book, declared God's righteous acts and judgments; now, he must prophesy "again"—reveal the contents of the "little book."

A Question: What were the contents of "the little book?" what does it reveal? Not tidings of mercy to a sinful world—this would not have grieved the aged seer. Not the judgment of the world—this was disclosed in the larger book, the book with seven seals. The "little book" does not directly concern so many people. It reveals the faithlessness and fate of a portion of Christ's church. This explains why the book was called "little," and why John was grieved when he read it. The contents are made known in chapters that follow.

From This Chapter Learn:

1. That the sea and the earth and all things therein belong to the Lord. By right of creation and by right of preservation, they are his. He has the right, therefore, to terminate all earthly affairs and this he will do at the appointed time.

2. That the afflictions of God's people are momentary. At the sounding of the seventh trumpet, or the end of the present age, they will find relief. (2 Cor. 4: 17, 18.)

3. That God's word is to be digested, assimilated, thoroughly mastered. Blessed is the man who gives himself to diligent study. (Psalm 1: 1, 2.)

4. That the word of God is both "sweet" and "bitter." In its disclosures of infinite compassion and promises of future blessedness, it is "sweet" indeed; but in its conviction of sin, rebukes, threats and fearful warnings, it is "bitter." Every portion, whether "sweet" or "bitter," was given for our good and eternal salvation.

5. That the lessons we derive from the Bible should be faithfully proclaimed. The gospel of Christ is not ours to hoard or to hide, but to share and to declare.

Memory Selection

"Take it, and eat it up; and it shall make thy belly bitter, but in thy mouth it shall be sweet." (Verse 9b.)

Daily Readings

Monday: Between the Sixth and Seventh Seals. (Rev. 7: 1-17.)
Tuesday: "The End of the World.'" (Matt. 13: 24-43.)
Wednesday: A Vision of Divine Glory. (Ezek. 1: 1-28.)
Thursday: "Son of Man, I Will Send Thee." (Ezek. 2: 1-27.)
Friday: "Son of Man, Eat this Roll." (Ezek. 3: 1-27.)
Saturday: An Oath Most Solemn. (Dan. 12: 1-13.)

For Class Discussion

1. What do we have between the sixth and seventh seals? the sixth and the seventh trumpets?

2. State briefly the contents of the lesson text. Into how many divisions does it fall? Name them.

3. In verses 1 and 2, describe the "strong angel." What of his origin, and the importance of his message?

4. What did he hold in his hand? What are the two characteristics of the book? What is the meaning of each?

5. Describe the angel's cry and reverberation that followed. What impulse came to John? With what prohibition?

6. In verse 5, describe the angel's position. What gesture did he make? To what oath did he give utterance?

7. What was John told to do with the book? What does this

mean? Was he obedient? What reaction followed his experience? Discuss.

8. After John ate the book, what was he told to do?

9. What were the contents of the book? Why do you answer as you do?

10. Quote the memory selection.

11. What practical lessons are suggested by the lesson?

INTERMEDIATE VISIONS—II
THE TEMPLE AND THE TWO WITNESSES
and
THE SEVENTH TRUMPET

Text: Rev. 11: 1-19   **Lesson XVI**

In chapter 10 we saw "the little book" in the hand of a "strong angel" and wondered concerning its contents. The contents are partly disclosed in chapter 11, which we now open for study. This chapter falls into three parts, namely: The temple; the two witnesses; and the sounding of the seventh trumpet. The first two parts are closely related; the third concludes the series of trumpet blasts, which was interrupted by the intermediate visions.

I. The Temple (Verses 1, 2)

1 **And there was given me a reed like unto a rod: and one said, Rise, and measure the temple of God, and the altar, and them that worship therein.** First, note the instruction given: "Rise, and measure," etc. The idea of measuring was taken from the Old Testament. (See Ezek. 10: 1-49; Zech. 2: 1-12.) God measures in order to keep, to preserve (Zech. 2: 5). Marking off a part of the temple is parallel to the sealing of the 144,000, chapter 7. Second, the instrument to be used: "A reed like unto a rod"—canon of Scripture. And third, the thing to be measured: "The temple"— sanctuary—representing the faithful church (1 Cor. 3: 16); "and the altar," the prayers; "and them that worship therein," or the true worshippers. 2 **And the court which is without the temple leave without, and measure it not for it hath been given unto the nations: and the holy city shall they tread under foot forty and two months.** First, note the prohibition:—John was told not to measure "the court," the temple area representing the unfaithful portion of the church. Second, the reason for the prohibition: It has fallen under the influence of "the nations," the spirit of the world, for "forty and two months" (three and one-half years), the entire period of the Christian dispensation. (Seven, the perfect number, seems to repre-

sent the long period of time from the beginning to the end. Three and one-half years, one-half of seven, represents the last of the two great dispensations.)

II. The Two Witnesses (Verses 3-13)

3 And I will give unto my two witnesses, and they shall prophesy a thousand two hundred and three score days, clothed in sackcloth. In the midst of the defection, God's witnesses appear. First, their number is sufficient (Deut. 19: 15; Matt. 18: 16). God often sent out his witnesses in pairs: Moses and Aaron; Elijah and Elisha; the disciples (Luke 10: 1). The two witnesses cannot be identified as individuals, but as the Lord's people in every age who declare and defend his truth. Second, the duration of their testimony is 1260 days (forty and two months, or three and one-half years), the entire period of the Christian age. God shall never be without witnesses. And third, they do their work in sadness. Not in radiant robes, but in robes of mourning ("sackcloth") do they fight. It isn't a light task to stand up against an evil world and condemn its sins. In the following verses we have representatives of the witnesses. **4 These are the two olive trees and the two candlesticks, standing before the Lord of the earth.** The olive trees supplied the candlesticks, the candlesticks diffused the light. The testimony of the witnesses shall be fed with streams of heavenly oil—the Holy Spirit. (Zech. 4.) **5 And if any man desireth to hurt them, fire proceedeth out of their mouth and devoureth their enemies; and if any man shall desire to hurt them, in this manner must he be killed. 6 These have the power to shut the heaven, that it rain not during the days of their prophecy: and they have power over the waters to turn them into blood, and to smite the earth with every plague, as often as they shall desire.** Note the power with which their testimony is borne. First, fire from their mouth. They consume their foes by the fire of truth they proclaim. (See 2 Kings 1: 10-12.) Second, they shut the heavens, as Elijah (1 Kings 17: 1; James 5: 16, 17.) Showers of mercy are closed to the men who oppose their testimony. Third, they turn water into blood, as Moses (Ex. 7). For rebellious men, blessings are turned into a curse. **7 And when they shall have finished their testimony, the beast that cometh up out of the abyss shall make war with them, and overcome them, and kill them.** The enemy that overcomes them is "the beast," a symbol of sin or Satan. The following verses depict the humiliation to which they are subjected. **8 And their dead bodies lie in the street of the great city, which spiritually is called Sodom and Egypt, where also their Lord was crucified.** Jerusalem, "the great city," represents the degenerate church. Like Sodom, she is corrupt: like Egypt, tyrannical. **9 And from among the peoples and tribes and tongues and nations do men look upon their dead bodies three days and a half, and suffer not their dead bodies to be laid in a tomb.** Those who have preached the gospel have suffered ridicule, persecution and humiliation during all ages. **10 And they that dwell on the earth rejoice over them, and make merry; and they shall send gifts one to another; because these two prophets tormented them that dwell on the earth.** The world and the degenerate church, having been "tormented" or disturbed by the preaching of the word, now congratulate themselves over their triumph. (See Luke 23: 12.) But the defeat of the witnesses "is only for the moment." **11 And after three days and a half the breath of life from God entered into them, and they stood upon their feet: and great fear fell upon them that beheld them. 12 And they heard a great voice from heaven saying unto them, Come up hither. And they went up into heaven in the cloud; and their enemies beheld them.** Having suffered with Christ, they shall also reign with him. Every defeat of a Christian is in appearance only. Though rejected, killed and humiliated before the world, like the Lord Jesus they shall rise and ascend. "Truth crushed to earth shall rise again." **13 And in that hour there was a great earthquake, and the tenth part of the city fell; and there were killed in the earthquake seven thousand persons.** Of those who deserved Divine judgment, none escaped. **And the rest were affrighted, and gave glory to the God of heaven.** Every triumph of the world is in appearance only, like the victory of the Jews over Jesus. The intention in the preceding verses is "to convey the idea that the church, in her witness for God, will experience opposition from the power of Satan, which will wax more and more formidable as time goes on, and result in the apparent triumph of the forces of evil. But the triumph will be brief; it will usher in the end and the final subjugation of the world."

III. The Seventh Trumpet: The Triumph (Verses 14-19)

14 The second Woe is past: behold, the third Woe cometh quickly. This is the last of the three woe-trumpets; also the last of the series of seven. (See 8: 3.) To the wicked, this is a trumpet of doom; to the righteous, a trumpet of joy. The ultimate defeat of the one and the ultimate triumph of the other are simultaneous.

15 And the seventh angel sounded; and there followed great voices in heaven, and they said, The kingdom of the world is become the kingdom of our Lord, and of his Christ: and he shall reign for ever and ever. The sounding of the last trumpet awakens heavenly voices which proclaim tidings of great joy. This announcement tells us that the battle of the ages—between right and wrong—is ended, resulting in the triumph of the right. The victory is complete—the usurper is ousted, shorn of his power. The victory is also permanent —the Lord shall "reign for ever and ever." (See 1 Cor. 15: 24-28.) **16 And the four and twenty elders, who sit before God on their thrones, fell upon their faces and worshipped God, 17 saying, We give thee thanks, O Lord God, the Almighty, who art and who wast; because thou hast taken thy great power, and didst reign. 18 And the nations were wroth, and thy wrath came—wrath met wrath—and the time of the dead to be judged, and the time to give their reward to thy servants the prophets, and to the saints, and to them that fear thy name, the small and the great; and to destroy them that destroy the earth.** No sooner is the great announcement made than we hear this outburst of thanksgiving, a son of deliverance. (See Ex. 15.) First, the singers are "the four and twenty elders," representatives of the glorified church, battle-scarred veterans. (See 4: 10, 11; 5: 8ff.) Their position is an exalted one: they "sit before God on their throne." Their attitude betokens reverence: for they "fell upon their faces." Second, the object of their praise is the "Lord God, the Almighty, who art and who wast." The familiar expression, "and to come" is omitted, because the Lord has now come. (See 1: 8.) Third, the ground of the praise: "Because thou hast taken thy great power, and didst reign." It is the joy of the saints that God reigns—they have nothing to fear. The manner in which he manifests his reigning power is pointed out: He shows his wrath; he judges—takes the destiny of men into his own hands; he rewards —no saint shall go unrewarded (Heb. 6: 10); he destroys them "that destroy the earth." This is retribution in kind. (See 2 Cor. 3: 17.) **19 And there was opened the temple of God that is in heaven; and there was seen in his temple the ark of his covenant; and there followed lightnings, and voices, and thunders, and an earthquake, and great hail.** This verse presents two contrasting scenes. First, God's sanctuary in heaven—"the secret place of the Most High." It was open for vision. "The ark of the covenant" is the pledge of God's faithfulness in saving his people. Second, a storm upon the earth. What a picture! Lightning playing upon a sky of darkness and gloom. Voices whose words are unrevealed. The rumbling of thunder which warn men of impending disaster. An earthquake which makes to tremble all earthly foundations. "And great hail," a symbol of God's wrath against sin. (See 16: 21; Heb. 12: 25-29.) Again, let it be remembered that it is the word-picture as a whole, not the various details, that should arrest our attention.

From This Chapter Learn:

1. That God measures men by his word. Those who meet the requirement, he preserves.

2. That the cause of righteousness on earth has defenders, strong and faithful.

3. That the cause of righteousness on earth has antagonists, strong and terrible.

4. That the defeat of the righteous is more apparent than real.

5. That the victory of the wicked is more apparent than real.

6. That the final defeat of the wicked and the final triumph of the righteous will be simultaneous.

Memory Selection

"The kingdom of the world is become the kingdom of our Lord, and of his Christ: and he shall reign for ever and ever." (Verse 15b.)

Daily Readings

Monday: "A Measuring Reed." (Ezek. 40: 1-49.)
Tuesday: "A Man with a Measuring Line." (Zech. 2: 1-13.)
Wednesday: "Ye Are a Temple." (1 Cor. 3: 1-23.)
Thursday: Olive Trees and a Candletstick. (Zech. 4: 1-14.)
Friday: A Song of Deliverance (Ex. 15: 1-27.)
Saturday: "A Kingdom that Cannot be Shaken." (Heb. 12: 1-29.)

For Class Discussion

1. Review briefly the contents of chapter 10. What can you say concerning the contents of "the little book?"

2. Into what three parts does chapter 11 fall?

3. In verse 1, what was John told to do? What is the temple? the altar? Who are the worshippers? What is the measuring reed?

4. What is the purpose of the measuring?

5. Was John forbidden to measure the court? Discuss.

6. What can you say of the two witnesses? their number? their identity?

7. What can you say of the power with which their testimony is borne? Discuss their momentary defeat, also their final victory.

8. What is the meaning of the seventh trumpet to the wicked? to the righteous?

9. What great announcement is made in verse 15? What outburst of thanksgiving followed?

10. Describe the contrasting scenes in verse 19.

11. Quote the memory selection.

12. What practical lessons are suggested in the chapter?

PART IV

The Enemies of the Church
(Rev. 12: 1-14: 20)
"A GREAT RED DRAGON"

Text: Rev. 12: 1-17   **Lesson XVII**

At this time we enter another section of the book of Revelation. (Chapters 12, 13 and 14.) In chapters 12 and 13 the great enemies of Christ and his church are brought forward under the personification of the dragon, the beast of the sea, and the beast of the land. In chapter 14 we have visions of encouragement, in which the Lamb and his followers are assured of ultimate triumph.

There is no chronological relation between this section and the preceding one. The book of Revelation is not a continuous history but a review of the struggle between sin and righteousness over and over under different aspects and under different symbols. In chapter 12 we have a picture of the first enemy of Christ and his church, the dragon, and the mighty conflict that ensued. Let us take a look at the three sub-topics, namely: Signs in heaven; war in heaven; and war on earth.

I. Signs in Heaven (Verses 1-6)

1 And a great sign was seen in heaven: a woman arrayed with the sun, and the moon under her feet, and upon her head a crown of twelve stars; 2 and she was with child; and she crieth out, travailing in birth, and in pain to be delivered. 3 And there was another sign in heaven: and behold a great red dragon, having seven heads and ten horns, and upon his heads seven diadems. 4 And his tail draweth the third part of the stars of heaven, and did cast them to the earth: and the dragon standeth before the woman that is about to be delivered, that when she is delivered he may devour her child. 5 And she was delivered of a son, a man child, literally, "A son, a male," who is to rule all the nations with a rod of iron: and her child was caught up unto God, and unto the throne. 6 And the woman fled into the wilderness, where she hath a place prepared of God, that there they may nourish her a thousand two hundred and threescore days. In this paragraph, two signs appear. One is a symbol of righteousness, the other of evil.

The first sign is a woman, arrayed in white, an emblem of righteousness. (See Gen. 1: 16.) Her crown reminds us of the church, her pregnancy of the virgin Mary, the child of Jesus. She is a pattern of the church. The birth of the child is a symbol of the birth of Jesus. The whole picture is an ideal one which precedes the actual.

The second sign is a dragon. A dragon has been described as "that fabulous monster of whom ancient poets told, as large in size, coiled like a snake, blood red in color, unsatiable in voracity, and ever athirst for human blood." He represents the evil spirit, the persecutor of Christ's church. Note in detail the points of description. (a) He is "red," the color of blood. He destroys men. (b) He has "seven heads and ten horns," i.e., he possesses all kinds of unholy power. (c) Upon his heads are "seven diadems"—marks of royalty. He is prince in his realm. (See Eph. 2: 2.) (d) His tail is an instrument of destruction. Men and, perhaps, angels (stars) are swayed by his influence. (e) The position he occupies: "Before the woman," etc. He tries desperately to destroy incarnate goodness in his very infancy. We are reminded of Pharaoh's efforts to destroy Moses (Ezek. 29: 3), and Herod's effort to destroy Jesus (Matt. 2: 16). But, like both Pharaoh and Herod, the dragon was "mocked" by the wisdom of God. At the ascension, Jesus "was caught up unto God, and unto his throne." The church of Christ escapes from the dragon, as the Israelites escaped from Pharaoh in the wilderness, to be guarded and nourished in time of trouble for 1260 days (three and one-half years), which is the entire period of the Christian dispensation. (See 1 Pet. 1: 1-5.)

II. War in Heaven (Verses 7-12)

7 **And there was war in heaven: Michael and his angels going forth to war with the dragon; and the dragon warred with his angels.** There is ever a contention between the forces that are evil and the forces that are Divine. This paragraph describes a decisive conflict. The combatants are named. Michael, the guardian of God's people (Dan. 10: 13, 21; Jude 9), is the agressor. As Christ's representative, he leads the forces of righteousness; the dragon leads the forces of evil. 8 **And they prevailed not, nor was their place found any more in heaven. 9 And the great dragon was cast down, the old serpent** (Gen. 3: 1), **he that is called the Devil** (adversary) **and Satan** (deceiver), **the deceiver of the whole world.** Here the identity of the great dragon is revealed. **He was cast down to the earth,** a lower spiritual state, **and his angels were cast down with him.** His army was utterly discomfited. The prince of this world was cast down. (See John 12: 31.) A Stronger than he entered the palace and seized from him "all his armour wherein he trusted, and divided his spoils."

10 **And I heard a great voice in heaven, saying, Now is come the salvation, and the power, and the kingdom of our God, and the authority of his Christ.** The victory is followed by a triumphant song, proclaiming the deliverance of man and the reign of God through his Son. (See Matt. 28: 18; Acts 2: 37, 38.) **For the accuser of our brethren is cast down, who accuseth them before our God day and night.** In these words we have a graphic delineation of the miserable victim and his evil work. 11 **And they overcame him because of the blood of the Lamb, and because of the word of their testimony; and they loved not their life even unto death.** This verse points out the triumphant weapons: First, "the blood of the Lamb," or the gospel (Rom. 1: 16); second, "the word of their testimony," or the truth they proclaimed (Heb. 4: 12); and third, their self-sacrificing love: for "they loved not their life even unto death." 12 **Therefore rejoice, O heavens, and ye that dwell in them. Woe for the earth and for the sea: because the devil is gone down unto you, having great wrath, knowing that he hath but a short time.** Infuriated at his defeat by the resurrection of Christ, and knowing that he has but a short time upon the earth until he shall be cast still lower (Rev. 20: 10), he concentrates his evil efforts.

III. War on Earth (Verses 13-17)

13 **And when the dragon saw that he was cast down to the earth, he persecuted the woman that brought forth the man child.** Defeated in his efforts against God in heaven, and foiled in his attack upon the man child—the Lord Jesus, the devil now directs his efforts against the woman—the Lord's church. This is the actual church, the church of history. His attacks against the church are not confined to any particular form of persecution, but includes persecution of the hand, of the tongue, and of the pen. 14 **And there were given to the woman the two wings of the great eagle, that she might fly into the wilderness unto her place, where she is nourished.** The escape of Israel from the bondage of Pharaoh, and her preservation in the wilderness, are referred to under the same figure (Ex. 19: 3, 4). "Her place" is "a place prepared of God." Though the church is in the world, it is not of the world. As Israel was nourished in the wilderness, so the church is nourished and sustained by bread from heaven (John 6) in her pilgrimage on the earth. **For a time** (one year), **and times** (two years), **and half a time** (half a year), **from the face of the serpent.** For three and one-half years, or the period of time covering the entire Christian era, the church is nourished and sustained. 15 **And the serpent cast out of his mouth after the woman water as a river, that he might cause her to be carried away by**

the stream. A flood frequently expresses overwhelming disaster. (See Psalm 69: 15; 90: 5.) The flood or the river of our text represents every form of destruction with which the devil endeavors to overwhelm the church of Christ. 16 **And the earth helped the woman, and the earth opened her mouth and swallowed up the river which the dragon cast out of his mouth.** "The earth," or the world, helped the woman because she had at this time become so much like the world. "When the church's tone and life are lowered by her yielding to the influence of the things of time, then the world, 'the earth,' is ready to hasten to her side. It offers her its friendship, courts alliances with her, praises her for the good order which she introduces, by arguments drawn from eternity, into the things of time, and swallows up the river which the dragon casts out of his mouth against her. When Christ's disciples are of the world, the world loves its own (John 15: 19)." (Milligan.) 17 **And the dragon waxed wroth with the woman, and went away to make war with the rest of her seed, that keep the commandments of God, and hold the testimony of Jesus.** A remnant ("the rest") was left. They were the "few names in Sardis that did not defile their garments" (Rev. 3: 4), "a remnant according to the election of grace" (Rom. 11: 5), "the seed which Jehovah hath blessed" (Isa. 61: 9). Leaving the degenerate portion of the church, the serpent went in pursuit of the remnant, the faithful few scattered over the face of the earth.

From This Chapter Learn:

1. That a perpetual warfare exists between good and evil, between God and Satan, between God's people and Satan's people. God's people are admonished to be sober, to be watchful. (See 1 Pet. 5: 8.)

2. That the "weapons of our warfare are not of the flesh" (2 Cor. 10: 4). We are to "take up the whole armour of God" (Eph. 6: 13-20). By means of the gospel of Christ, the sword of the Spirit, and a life of devotion we shall overcome.

3. That, during the period of temptation and persecution the Lord has a place prepared for his people. There he sustains them. (See Psalm 91: 1.)

4. That the devil makes war, not against the degenerate church or the degenerate Christian, but against the faithful Christian—the one that keeps the commandments of God, and holds the testimony of Jesus.

Daily Readings

Monday: The Old Serpent. (Gen. 3: 1-24.)
Tuesday: "Michael Your Prince." (Dan. 10: 1-21; Jude 9.)
Wednesday: Effort to Destroy Moses. (Ex. 1: 1-22; 2: 1-10.)
Thursday: Effort to·Destroy Jesus. (Matt. 2: 1-23.)
Friday: "I Bare You on Eagles' Wings." (Ex. 19: 1-25.)
Saturday: Bread from Heaven. (Ex. 16: 1-36; John 6: 1-59.)

For Class Discussion

1. What section of the book do we now enter? What do we find in this section?

2. In verses 1-6, what two signs appear? Of what is the radiant woman a symbol? the great red dragon? the man child?

3. Describe the woman, the dragon, the efforts of the dragon. How were the efforts of the dragon mocked?

4. Describe the war in heaven, as depicted in verses 7-12. Who are the combatants?

5. What was the outcome of this war? What song followed the victory? Whence did it come? By what weapons was the battle won?

6. Describe the war on earth, as depicted in verses 13-17. Who was the persecutor? the persecuted? Where did the woman find refuge? How was she there sustained? by what means? and how long?

7. What does the "water as a river," in verse 15, represent? Why did the "earth" help the woman?

8. In verse 17, with whom did the dragon make war? Who are "the rest of her seed"? How are they described?

9. What lessons are suggested by the lesson?

THE TWO BEASTS

Text: Rev. 13: 1-18   **Lesson XVIII**

The presiding genius over all forces of evil is the "great red dragon," unto whom we were introduced in chapter 12. He is the archenemy of Christ, of Christ's church, of all mankind. In a preeminent sense, he is the antichrist. He has been identified as the devil, as Satan, as the old serpent, as "the prince of the power of the air," that "worketh in the sons of disobedience."

Though Satan is the archenemy of mankind and though he is responsible for much of the misery and mischief in the world, his responsibility in the realm of darkness is not an unshared one. In chapter 13, two other enemies are portrayed as agents and coworkers of Satan—one under the figure of the beast of the sea, the other under the figure of the beast of the land.

I. The Beast of the Sea (Verses 1-10)

1 **And he** (the dragon) **stood upon the sand of the sea. And I saw a beast coming up out of the sea, having ten horns and seven heads.** Perhaps, the horns are mentioned first, because they were first seen as the beast emerged from the water. **And on his horns ten diadems, and upon his heads names of blasphemy. 2 And the beast which I saw was like unto a leopard, and his feet were as the feet of a bear, and his mouth as the mouth of a lion; and the dragon gave him his power, and his throne, and great authority. 3 And I saw one of his heads as though it had been smitten unto death; and his deathstroke was healed: and the whole world wondered after the beast; 4 and they worshipped the dragon, because he gave his authority unto the beast; and they worshipped the beast, saying, Who is like unto the beast? and who is able to make war with him? 5 and there was given to him a mouth speaking great things and blasphemies; and there was given to him authority to continue forty and two months. 6 And he opened his mouth for blasphemies against God, to blaspheme his name, and his tabernacle, even them that dwell in the heaven. 7 And it was given unto him to make war with the saints, and to overcome them; and there was given to him authority over every tribe and people and tongue and nation. 8 And all that dwell on the earth shall worship him, every one whose name hath not been written from the foundation of the world in the book of life of the Lamb that hath been slain. 9 If any man hath an ear, let him hear. 10 If any man is for captivity, into captivity he goeth: if any man shall kill with the sword, with the sword must he be killed.** If any man is determined to sin, he shall become a slave of sin. He shall reap what he sows. **Here is the patience and the faith of the saints.**

Of what is the beast of the sea a symbol? First, he is a symbol of a kingdom or a power or an influence in the world. "Out of the sea" of a restless people he came. Of the spirit of restlessness and commotion he was born. A horn denotes power; the "ten horns" of the beast denote a plentitude of power. The head is the controlling and guiding part of the body—that part to which the members of the body are subject. The "seven heads" represent the world-powers by which God's people had been persecuted in the past or were to be persecuted in the future—Egypt, Assyria, Babylon, Medo-Persia, Greece, Rome and the seventh power yet to be identified. The "diadems" are marks of royalty. Second, he is a symbol of an evil power. Toward God he is arrogant, as indicated by the "names of blasphemy" he bore. He claims for himself the authority which belongs only to the Almighty. Toward God's children he is brutish. Leopard-like, he is crafty and cruel; bear-like, he is slow and relentless in tread; lion-like, he is strong and vicious. He is a perfect beast of prey. Toward the dragon he is friendly and submissive. Satan "gave him his power, and his throne, and great authority." Third, he is a symbol of a power of amazing vitality, as indicated in verse 3. The sixth head (the Roman Empire) was smitten, but the beast survived. (Rev. 17: 8-11.) It is with the beast in his resurrection state that we are to deal, as the world wondered after him after his resurrection. The period of his duration is "forty and two months," the full time of the Christian era. Fourth, he is a symbol of an idolized power. His votaries ascribe to him the praise which is due God alone, as pointed out in verse 4. (See Ex. 15: 11; Ps. 35: 10; 71: 19.) The four divisions—"every tribe and people and tongue and nation"—represent the scope of his influence. And fifth, he is a symbol of a destructive power; hence, the necessity of the admonition of verses 9 and 10. He captivates and kills all who come within his reach. Here is the opportunity for the saints to manifest their faith and patience.

The beast of the sea is not any human government. He possesses characteristics never possessed by any such power, namely, his universal influence and amazing vitality. He is a travesty of the Lord Jesus. Like Jesus, he represents an unseen power; like Jesus, he had a death and resurrection; like Jesus, he has a throng of worshippers; like Jesus, his influence knows no national boundary. He is the personification of the spirit of the present evil world. (See 1 Cor. 2: 12; Jas. 4: 4; 1 John 2: 15, 16.) Like the beast of the sea, this spirit comes up out of the midst of discontented people; like the beast, it is passion-ruled; like the beast, it possesses an arrogance which divorces man from God; like the beast, it has an amazing vitality—it is found at all times and places; like the beast, it is destructive in nature.

II. The Beast of the Land (Verses 11-18)

11 And I saw another beast coming up out of the earth; and he had two horns like unto a lamb, and he spake as a dragon. 12 And he exerciseth all the authority of the first beast in his sight. And he maketh the earth and them that dwell therein to worship the first beast, whose death-stroke was healed. 13 And he doeth great signs, that he should even make fire to come down out of heaven upon the earth in the sight of men. 14 And he deceiveth them that dwell on the earth by reason of the signs which was given him to do in the sight of the beast; saying to them that dwell on the earth, that they should make an image to the beast who hath the stroke of the sword and lived. 15 And it was given unto him to give breath to it, even to the image of the beast, that the image of the beast should both speak, and cause that as many as should not worship the image of the beast should be killed. 16 And he causeth all, the small and the great, and the rich and the poor, and the free and the bond, that there be given them a mark on their right hand, or upon their forehead; 17 and that no man should be able to buy or to sell, save he that hath the mark, even the name of the beast or the number of his name. 18 Here is wisdom. He that hath understanding, let him count the number of the beast; for it is the number of a man and his number is Six hundred and sixty six.

Concerning this beast, let us make some observations. First, his origin. He came "up out of the earth." To the Hebrew mind "the sea," in its barrenness and restlessness, was a symbol of the heathen world; "the earth," in its quiet and fruitfulness, was a symbol of the Jewish nation—God's chosen. Hence, the beast had his origin among God's people—the church. Second, his characteristics. He is harmless in appearance, having "horns like unto a lamb," but speaks like the devil. Hence, he is a deceptive influence, a hypocritical power. (See Matt. 7: 15.) Third, the authority he exercises. (Verses 12-17.) He is a slave of the first beast—possesses the same spirit, the same kind of character. He exercises "all the authority of the first beast," but how? (a) He causes carnally minded people "to worship the first beast." Here we have religion doing service for the spirit of the world. (b) He works "great signs," the purpose of which is to deceive the elect. (See Matt. 24: 24; 2 Thess. 2: 2-10.) (c) He orders an image erected to the first beast. He idolizes the world and the things therein. "Nothing is worthy to be worshipped," says he, "but that which is visible and tangible." He animates the image—tries to make a corpse appear life-like. He gives it power to persecute. Deception is tried first; if deception fails, then come blood and violence. Violence has always been a method of false religion. (d) He brands his own, as a master his slave—on the hand and on the forehead. All who do not subscribe to carnal religion are cut off from social and commercial intercourse. And fourth, the man and his number—666. The mark, the name and the number are all identical. God's servants are never stamped with a number, but with a name. (See Rev. 3: 12.) "The man," therefore, is not God's servant. The number of the man falls short of the Divine. Among the Jews there was a doom upon the number 6, even when it stood alone: for it fell hopelessly short of the sacred number 7. The number 6, therefore, is the world's number. The number 666 represents worldliness at its zenith, "expressing all that it is possible for human wisdom and power, when directed by an evil spirit, to achieve." The man cannot be identified as an individual, but as a type, as a kind.

Of what is the beast of the earth a symbol? An influence or a power in the world. He is an evil power: for a beast is a symbol of evil. He is a deceptive power. He possesses the same character of the beast of the sea, but a different garb. He represents evil in the highest state of refinement, the most perfect counterfeit of goodness, the spirit of the world clothed in mild manners. He is the spirit of carnal religion, like the religion that opposed the Savior during the days of his flesh and slew him, a religion that is ready to resort to physical violence to attain its end, a religion that seeks to substitute empty forms for spirituality, that insists on walking by sight and not by faith. The beast of the land is the false prophet, the degenerate church, the apostate Christian.

From This Chapter Learn:

1. That the spirit of this world, symbolized by the beast of the sea, is an enemy of Christ's church. In three forms it is manifested: "The lust of the flesh—sensuality; "the lust of the eyes"—covetousness; and "the vainglory of life"—the desire to dominate, to rule, to control, to be elevated to a position above one's fellows. (1 John 2: 15, 16.)

2. That false religion (the religion of Christ corrupted by the spirit of this world), symbolized by the beast of the land, is also a deadly enemy of the church. It behooves the Christian to love the Lord supremely and to preserve the purity of true religion, as revealed in the New Testament. (See Jas. 1: 19-27.)

Daily Readings

Monday: "Four Great Beasts." (Dan. 7: 1-28.)
Tuesday: A Woman and a Beast. (Rev. 17: 1-18.)
Wednesday: "Love Not the World." (1 John 2: 1-29.)
Thursday: "Guard Yourselves from Idols." (1 John 5: 1-21.)
Friday: "Pure Religion and Undefiled." (James 1: 1-27.)
Saturday: "The Man of Sin." (2 Thess. 2: 1-17.)

For Class Discussion

1. Review briefly the preceding chapter, connecting it with the present chapter.

2. Who is the presiding genius over all forces of evil?

3. In chapter 12, what two beasts are linked with the dragon of chapter 13?

4. Describe the beast of the sea. What is represented by his horns, his heads, his diadems? From whom does this beast receive his power?

5. Of what is the beast of the sea a symbol? Discuss freely. Does he represent any human government? Give reasons for your answer.

6. Discuss the beast of the land. Show his relation to the beast of the sea.

7. Is the beast of the land an evil power? a deceptive power? Give reasons for your answers.

8. Of what is the beast of the land a symbol? Why do you answer as you do?

9. Make a practical application of the assignment, showing the relation of the two beasts to evil forces now at work around us.

VISIONS OF TRIUMPH

Text: Rev. 14: 1-20   Lesson XIX

The Lord never keeps his people too long in the shadows. At

intervals he removed the cloud and allows golden rays to fall upon them. After the horrible convulsions depicted in chapter 6 came the glorious vision of the redeemed in heaven. In chapters 12 and 13 we saw the fierce enemies of the church and the deadly conflict that followed. And now, in chapter 14, by way of contrast and to encourage the church to resist her foes to the end with the assurance of a glorious triumph, two scenes are depicted: One showing the future blessedness of the saints, the other God's vengeance on their enemies.

I. The Lamb on Mount Zion (Verses 1-5)

1 **And I saw, and behold, the Lamb standing.** After looking upon the dragon and the two beasts, what a relief to look upon the Lamb! He has been slain. Now he is risen. Undisturbed by the raving of the three foes, he stands, firm, calm and self-possessed. **On the mount Zion,** God's dwelling place (Psalm 9: 11); the mount of Divine love (Psalm 78: 68); the place whence comes salvation (Psalm 14: 7); the holy hill upon which God sets his king (Psalm 2: 6, 7); the place to which the ransomed of the Lord shall return (Isa. 35: 10). It is the city of the living God (Heb. 12: 22-24), a place lifted above the pagan world. **And with him a hundred and forty and four thousand, having his name, and the name of his Father, written on their foreheads.** These were the Lamb's attendants, a number which represents God's elect. (Rev. 7: 1-8.) Their fellowship was not with their foes but the Redeemer. They did not bear the mark, the name and the number of the beast; but the names of the Father and the Son. (Rev. 13: 18.) 2 **And I heard a voice from heaven as the voice of many waters, and as the voice of a great thunder: and the voice which I heard was as the voice of harpers harping with their harps: 3 and they sang as if it were a new song before the four living creatures and the elders: and no man could learn the song save the hundred and forty and four thousand, even they that had been purchased out of the earth.** Concerning the wonderful voice that John heard, let us make some observations. First, it came "from heaven." It must have been the voice of angels and glorified saints. Second, it was musical. As there was beauty for the eye, there was melody for the ear. Like "a voice of many waters," the melody was uninterrupted. At times it swelled into a volume "as the voice of a great thunder," then sank into a strain so soft that it resembled the music of harps. Majesty and sweetness were its characteristics. Third, it was vocal—a song of victory over the three enemies. It was never sung before, because such a conflict had never been fought before. Hence, it was "new." Only the church

could understand or interpret. This is true because she was
heavenly-minded. She alone was familiar with heaven's language.
**4 These are they that were not defiled with women; for they are
virgins,** i.e., they were virgin souls who had not bowed to the beast
or to his image. They were not guilty of spiritual fornication. To
the Bridegroom, to whom they had been joined in spiritual wed-lock,
they had been true. **These are they that follow the Lamb whither-
soever he goeth.** They had not wondered after the beast (Rev. 13:
3), but had followed the Lamb in his humiliation, work, suffering,
death, resurrection and ascension. **These were purchased from
among men, to be the firstfruits unto God and unto the Lamb.** The
idea of "firstfruits" in this place is not so much that of priority as
superiority. (See James 1: 18.) **5 And in their mouth was found no
lie.** They were unlike the beast of the land, who made great pre-
tentions. **They are without blemish.** They were like the Lamb
which had been slain. (See 1 Pet. 1: 19.)

II. The Harvest and Vintage (Verses 6-20)

This portion of the chapter consists of seven parts. Each of the
first three and each of the last three parts is introduced by an
angel. The fourth or central part is occupied by one "like unto a
son of man."

First: The Angel of the "Everlasting Gospel"

**6 And I saw another angel flying in mid heaven, having eternal
good tidings to proclaim unto them that dwell on the earth, and
unto ever nation and tribe and tongue and people; 7 and he saith
with a great voice, Fear God, and give him glory; for the hour of his
judgment is come: and worship him that made the heaven and the
earth and the sea and fountains of waters.** The angel descends
from heaven with a world-wide message, leaving the wicked world
without excuse. The idea in these verses is to emphasize the cer-
tainty of the coming judgment. As a preliminary to this, the gospel
is proclaimed to all nations, in accordance with the Master's words.
(Matt. 24: 14; 28: 18, 19.)

Second: The Angel of Doom

**8 And another, a second angel, followed, saying, Fallen, fallen
is Babylon the great,** which is identified with the harlot or the
degenerate church. It is interesting to note that her fall precedes
the fall of heathendom. (See 1 Pet. 4: 17.) **That hath made all the
nations to drink of the wine of the wrath of her fornication.** The
reason for her fall is here assigned. She had been untrue to Christ,

the Bridegroom. She had corrupted the world with her false doctrine and life.

Third: **The Angel of Warning**

9 **And another angel, a third, followed them, saying with a great voice, If any man worshippeth the beast and his image, and receiveth a mark on his forehead, or upon his hand.** This is mark of identification—the character of the ungodly. 10 **He also shall drink of the wine of the wrath of God, which is prepared unmixed in the cup of his anger; and he shall be tormented with fire and brimstone in the presence of the Lamb; and the smoke of their torment goeth up for ever and ever; and they have no rest day and night, they that worship the beast and his image, and whoso receiveth the mark of his name.** The adherents of the beast are to be held responsible for their deeds and punished accordingly. Their punishment is a just and an inevitable retribution—because they had made the nations drunk, God shall make them drunk—drunk with the wine of his wrath. It is "unmixed" with mercy.

Parenthetical Words

12 **Here is the patience of the saints, they that keep the commandments of God, and the faith of Jesus.** The patience of the saints is manifested in maintaining the conflict with the forces of evil and in waiting for the due retribution which will overtake them. 13 **And I heard a voice from heaven saying, Write, Blessed are the dead who die in the Lord from henceforth: yea, saith the Spirit, that they may rest from their labors; for their works follow with them.** The dangers to which the saints are daily exposed from the beast and his image called forth from the aged seer these strong words of encouragement.

Fourth: **ONE "LIKE UNTO A SON OF MAN"**

14 **And I saw, and behold, a white cloud; and on the cloud I saw one sitting like unto a son of man.** This is the Lord Jesus. He occupies the central position in the drama. As the all-victorious one, he presides over the harvest of the world. **Having on his head a golden crown,** a symbol of victory as well royalty, **and in his hand a sharp sickle.** He is a reaper.

Fifth: **The Angel of the Harvest**

15 **And another angel came from the temple,** the innermost sanctuary, the very presence of God, **crying with a great voice to him that sat on the cloud, Send forth thy sickle and reap: for the hour to reap is come: for the harvest of the earth is ripe,** for salvation.

16 And he that sat on the cloud cast his sickle upon the earth; and the earth was reaped. Responding to the "great voice," the reaper reaped, gathering the golden grain of the harvest into the garner of eternal security. All the faithful, without the loss of even one, shall be saved.

Sixth: The Angel of the Vintage

17 And another angel came forth out from the temple which is in heaven, he also having a sharp sickle. This is the angel of the vintage. Like the angel of the harvest, he came from the presence of God. As the harvest of the good was gathered by the Lord himself, the vintage of the wicked by his angel. "The ministry of mercy is the Lord's chosen office; the ministry of wrath his stern necessity." (See Matt. 13: 41, 42.)

Seventh: The Angel of Fire

18 And another angel came out from the altar, he that hath power over fire. The altar represents the prayers of the saints for judgment on the wicked. (See Rev. 6: 9, 10; 8: 3.) The angel here has power over the fire of God's avenging wrath. (See 2 Thess. 1: 7-9.) **And he called with a great voice to him that had the sickle, saying, Send forth the sharp sickle, and gather the clusters of the vine of the earth; for her grapes are ripe,** for crushing. **19 And the angel cast his sickle into the earth, and gathered the vintage of the earth, and cast it into the winepress, the great winepress, of the wrath of God. 20 And the winepress was trodden without the city, and there came out blood from the winepress, even unto the bridles of the horses, as far as a thousand and six hundred furlongs.** Responding to the "great voice" that called, the angel gathered the vintage of the earth—the wicked were punished. First, note the nature of the punishment—it was a crushing. Second, the place of it —"without the city." The ungodly shall suffer without the gate of the holy city. Third, the horror of it—"there came out blood," etc. And fourth, the extent of it—"as far as a thousand and six hundred furlongs." Four, a world number, is multiplied by itself to express intensity, then by one hundred, a number associated with evil in this book.

From This Chapter Learn:

1. That the Redeemer and the redeemed are eternal associates. Together they shall stand on mount Zion.

2. That music is love's language. Heaven is its source. A song was never heard from hell. From hell come sighs and groans.

3. That the dead who die in the Lord have the assurance of peace and rest.

4. That, for the followers of Christ, the end of the present age is a time of golden harvest, a time of ingathering.

5. That, for the ungodly, the end of the present age is a time of vintage—a time of crushing.

Memory Selection

"Blessed are the dead who die in the Lord from henceforth: yea, saith the Spirit, that they may rest from their labors; for their works follow with them." (Verse 13b.)

Daily Readings

Monday: "The City of the Living God." (Heb. 12: 1-29.)
Tuesday: The Return of the Ransomed. (Isa. 35: 1-10.)
Wednesday: The Sealing of the 144,000 (Rev. 7: 1-8.)
Thursday: The Parable of the Sower. (Matt. 13: 1-23.)
Friday: The Parable of the Tares. (Matt. 13: 24-43.)
Saturday: "Brimstone and Fire." (Gen. 19: 1-38.)

For Class Discussion

1. What is the relation between this chapter and the two preceding chapters?

2. Review briefly chapters 12 and 13. Who is the red dragon? What is represented by the beast of the sea? the beast of the land?

3. What beautiful vision do we have in chapter 14, verses 1-5? Who is the Lamb? Where is he standing? Who are his attendants? What voice did John hear from heaven? What did it resemble?

4. Of what do we have a vision in verses 6-20? How many parts do we find in this section? By whom are the first three and the last three parts introduced? Who occupies the central part of the drama?

5. What announcement is made by the first angel? the second? the third? What consolation for the saints is embedded in verses 12 and 13?

6. Describe the vision depicted in verses 14, 15 and 16. Who is the reaper? Who does the harvest represent?

7. Describe the vintage of the earth as given in verses 17-20. Who is represented by the grapes?

8. What practical lessons are taught?

PART V

THE SEVEN BOWLS

Text: Rev. 15: 1-16: 21   **Lesson XX**

In chapter 15 we have an introduction to a series of seven plagues. In chapter 16 these plagues are executed. Because the two chapters are so closely related we include both of them in one lesson.

Introduction (15:1-8)

1 And I saw another sign in heaven, great and marvelous, seven angels having seven plagues, which are the last, for in them is finished the wrath of God. The judgments of the bowls seem to be a recapitulation of what has been prophecied in the visions of the seals and the trumpets. But the recapitulation is more than a repetition. The idea contained in the vision of the seals and trumpets is strengthened and set forth more forcibly in conformity with verse 1 in which we are reminded that in the plagues of the bowls God's wrath "is finished."

2 And I saw as it were a sea of glass mingled with fire; and them that came off victorious from the beast, and from his image, and from the number of his name, standing by the sea of glass, having harps of God. What the harps symbolize is seen in the following verse. **3 And they sing the song of Moses the servant of God, and the song of the Lamb, saying, Great and marvelous are thy works, O Lord God, the Almighty; righteous and true are thy ways, thou King of the ages. 4 Who shall not fear, O Lord, and glorify thy name? for thou only art holy; for all nations shall come and worship before thee; for thy righteous acts have been made manifest.** The glassy sea mingled with fire, by which they stood, indicates the trials through which they had passed and by which they had been purified. (See 1 Pet. 1: 6, 7.) The figure reminds us of the deliverance of Israel from Pharaoh. (Ex. 14.) There were a triumphant people, therefore a happy people. Their song reveals their identity: for they sang the song of Moses and of the Lamb. They came from both the Jewish and the Christian dispensation. The power, the holiness and the justice of God are the grand theme. No matter what horrors may descend, they are secure.

5 And after these things I saw, and the temple of the tabernacle of the testimony in heaven was opened: 6 and there came out from the temple the seven angels that had the seven plagues, arrayed with precious stone, pure and bright, and girt about their

breasts with golden girdles. **7 And one of the four living creatures gave unto the seven angels seven golden bowls full of the wrath of God who liveth for ever and ever.** **8 And the temple was filled with smoke from the glory of God, and from his power; and none was able to enter into the temple, till the seven plagues of the seven angels should be finished.** In these verses the seven angels to whom we were introduced in verse 1 are described. Let us note: 1. Whence they came: "From the temple," the holy of holies, the dwelling place of God. They came, therefore, at God's bidding. "The testimony"— tables of stone—bears witness to the holiness and justice of God's government. 2. Their dress: They were "arrayed with precious stone," etc. This means that they were priestly angels, ready to do service at the command of the Almighty. 3. Their mission: They "had the seven plagues." This indicates that they were minister's of divine wrath. The action of the "living creatures" in verse 7 admitted the propriety of the judgment to be executed. The time is one of horror and all outward things correspond. Smoke from the glory of God filled the temple. (See Ex. 19: 18; 40: 34ff; 1 Kings 8: 10, 11; Isa. 6: 1-4.)

I. The First Six Bowls (16: 1-12)

1 And I heard a great voice out of the temple, saying to the seven angels, Go ye, and pour out the seven bowls of the wrath of God into the earth. The priestly angels were standing in readiness, but nothing could be done without a divine command. In verse 1 the command was given and the response was immediate.

2 And the first went, and poured out his bowl into the earth; and it became a noisome and grievous sore upon the men that had the mark (character) **of the beast, and that worshipped his image,** i.e., the things that bore his resemblance. By this we are reminded of the two former plagues: The sixth plague of Egypt which affected the people of that land (Ex. 9: 8ff); and of the plague of the first trumpet which affected lower creation (Rev. 8: 7). The plague of the first bowl affected men—the beast worshippers, carnally minded men.

3 And the second poured out his bowl into the sea; and it became blood as of a dead man; and every living soul died, even the things that were in the sea. This judgment recalls a milder visitation of Egypt. (Ex. 7: 17-21.) In a former vision a similar judgment had fallen upon a third part of the sea (Rev. 8: 8, 9), but now the whole. Note the ascending climax.

4 And the third poured out his bowl into the rivers and the

fountains of the waters; and it became blood. 5 And I heard the angel of the waters saying, Righteous art thou, who art and who wast, thou Holy One, because thou didst thus judge; 6 for they poured out the blood of saints and prophets, and blood hast thou given them to drink: they are worthy. This is retribution in kind—blood for blood. 7 And I heard the altar saying, Yea, O Lord God, the Almighty, true and righteous are thy judgments. In the Egyptian plague only the waters of that country were smitten. (Ex. 8: 10, 11.) But here we have the climax—all waters are smitten. The justice of this plague was acknowledged by the angel of the element in question, also by the altar which echoed the angel's voice. (See Rev. 6: 9, 10; 8: 3; 14: 18.)

8 And the fourth poured out his bowl upon the sun; and it was given unto it to scorch men with fire. 9 And men were scorched with great heat: and they blasphemed the name of God who hath the power over these plagues; and they repented not to give him glory. The beneficient sun was smitten with a curse to torture sinful man. That which had been created for a comfort became a means of punishment. The effect: Pain in the body, rebellion in the heart. Afflictions, if they do not melt, will harden the sinner.

10 And the fifth poured out his bowl upon the throne of the beast; and his kingdom was darkened; and they gnawed their tongues for pain, 11 and they blasphemed the God of heaven because of their pains and their sores; and they repented not of their works. The throne, the center of influence, which had been set up in arrogance and opposition to God's throne, is reached. Resulting from this came the following: First, darkness (Ex. 10: 21ff.) When men prefer darkness to light, God humors them. Second, pain. This is rendered more intense by the darkness. Third, blasphemy. Men blamed God for that which their own sins had brought. And fourth, impenitence and hardness of heart.

12 And the sixth poured out his bowl upon the great river, the river Euphrates; and the water thereof was dried up, that the way might be made ready for the kings that came from the sunrising. The action of the sixth angel prepared the way for the assembling of a mighty host. Note their royalty. They are "kings"—every one of them. (See Rev. 1: 6; 1 Pet. 2: 5, 9.) They came from the "sunrising"—the origin of light and hope (Rev. 7: 1; Matt. 2: 1). They remind us "of the remnant of the Israel of God as they returned from all places whither they had been led captive." They symbolize the forces of righteousness.

II. An Intermediate Vision (Verses 13-16)

13 **And I saw coming out of the mouth of the dragon, and out of the mouth of the beast, and out of the mouth of the false prophet, three unclean spirits, as it were frogs:** 14 **for they are spirits of demons, working signs; which go forth unto the kings of the whole world, to gather them together unto the war of the great day of God the Almighty.** The coming of the "kings from the sunrising" under the leadership of the King of kings was a challenge to the three anti-Christian powers. They accepted it and sent forth their "spirits" or apostles, unclean and noisy like frogs, to assemble the forces of evil. The origin of the apostles reveals their nature and identity. "Out of the mouth of the dragon" (the devil) came the apostle of infidelity; "out of the mouth of the beast" came the apostle of worldliness; "out of the mouth of the false prophet" came the apostle of false religion. 15 **(Behold, I come as a thief. Blessed is he that watcheth, and keepeth his garments, lest he walk naked, and they see his shame.** The trend of events alarm the brethren. Therefore the narrative is interrupted that Jesus may warn and console.) 16 **And they gathered them together into the place which is called in Hebrew, Ar-Magedon.** The word, Ar-Magedon, is compound derived from the Hebrew, meaning the mountain of Megiddo. The plain of Megiddo (or Esdraelon) was famous for great slaughters. (See Judges 4, 5; 2 Chron. 35.) There is no such place as Ar-Magedon. The name is symbolic. It signifies a conflict—not a carnal, but a spiritual conflict. It is the final and supreme effort of the powers of wickedness to overthrow the cause of Christ.

III. The Seventh Bowl (Verses 17-21)

17 **And the seventh poured out his bowl upon the air; and there came forth a great voice out of the temple, from the throne, saying, It is done:** 18 **and there were lightenings, and voices, and thunders; and there was a great earthquake, such as was not since there were men upon the earth, so great an earthquake, so mighty.** 19 **And the great city was divided into three parts, and the cities of the nations (Gentiles) fell: and Babylon the great was remembered in the sight of God, to give unto her the cup of the wine of the fierceness of his wrath.** 20 **And every island fled away, and the mountains were not found.** 21 **And great hail, every stone about the weight of a talent, cometh down out of heaven upon men: and men blasphemed God because of the plague of hail; for the plague thereof is exceeding great.** This action of the seventh angel, also the last, affected the air, including Satan, "the prince of the power of the air." (Eph. 2: 2.) This is followed by four things which are called "great." First, "A great

voice," declaring, "It is done"—the world's history finished. Second, "A great earthquake," without parallel, attended with lightnings, voices, and thunders. Third, the fall of "the great city," which is Babylon, the corrupt church. Heathendom, "the cities of the Gentiles," also fell. And fourth, "Great hail," the stones weighing more than 50 pounds each, another symbol of God's wrath. Because of this, men blasphemed God, showing that the time of their destruction was fully ripe.

From These Chapters Learn:

1. That many are the plagues that descend upon sinful men; but some day will come the final, the ultimate, the plague of all plagues which will shut the wicked within walls of eternal darkness where pain gnaws the heart.

2. That those who walk through the sea of trials and emerge victorious on the other side will have a beautiful song to sing. They will sing the "sweet song of deliverance." Heaven is a land of song. In that fair country the voice of mourning is never heard.

3. That the battle of Ar-Magedon is a spiritual warfare, raging in the hearts of men (1 Tim. 6: 12; Eph. 6: 10ff.) In the life of the individual, it means the decisive, the turning point of life.

4. That the reverses of sinful men should but do not always cause them to repent. When afflictions do not melt the heart, they harden it.

Memory Selection

"Great and marvelous are thy works, O Lord God, the Almighty; righteous and true are thy ways, thou King of the ages." (15: 3b.)

Daily Readings

Monday: The Hand of Deliverance. (Ex. 14: 1-31.)
Tuesday: Song of Moses. (Ex. 15: 1-27.)
Wednesday: "The Proof of Your Faith." (1 Pet. 1: 1-25.)
Thursday: "The Glory of Jehovah." (Ex. 40: 1-38.)
Friday: On the Plains of Esdraelon. (Judges 4, 5.)
Saturday: When Josiah was slain. (2 Chron. 35.)

For Class Discussion

1. What is the lesson subject? In what two chapters is our lesson found? Why do we study them together?

2. Quote verse 1, chapter 15, and comment on the same.

3. In verses 2-4 what vision do we have? What did John see? hear?

4. In verses 5-8, what three-point description of the seven angels is given?

5. Describe the first six bowls of chapter 16, verses 1-12. What is the significance of each?

6. What intermediate vision is depicted in verses 13-16? What can you say of the battle of Ar-Magedon?

7. In the seventh and last bowl, what four "great" things are specified?

8. What practical lessons do we glean from the assignment?

PART VI

"Babylon the Great"
(Rev. 17: 1-18: 24)

BABYLON DESCRIBED

Text: Rev. 17: 1-18   **Lesson XXI**

The lesson before us points out an evil of a certain type under the symbolism of an infamous woman. Those who are familiar with the Old Testament, especially the prophetic portions, will recall how often the terms "adultery" and "fornication" are employed. In Isa. 1: 21; Jer. 2: 20; 3: 1 and in other places, these terms are used to describe God's apostate people—those people who had been joined to him in covenant relationship only to break the marriage vow of faithfulness. "As fornication and adultery are forms of false affection, and are the prostitution of the most sacred part of our nature to alien purposes, so the alienation of the heart from God, and the departure of the church from fidelity to him, is a violation of the most sacred ties, and is the leaguing of the heart in a false alliance, which is odious to our God." (Clemance.)

Chapter 17 begins with "the mystery of the woman," continues with "the beast that carried her," and concludes by pointing out the relation between the two.

I. The Woman (Verses 1-6)

1 **And there came one of the seven angels that had the seven bowls,** reminding us of the close relationship between this lesson and the seven bowls, **and spake with me, saying, Come hither, I will show thee the judgment of the great harlot that sitteth upon many waters; 2 with whom the kings of the earth committed fornication, and they that dwell in the earth were made drunken with the wine of her fornication. 3 And he carried me away in the Spirit into a wilderness: and I saw a woman sitting upon a scarlet-colored beast, full of names of blasphemy, having seven heads and ten horns.** "The seven heads denote universality of (earthly) dominion, and the ten horns denote plentitude of power." (Plummer.) 4 **And the woman was arrayed in purple and scarlet, and decked with gold and precious stone and pearls, having in her hand a golden cup full of abominations, even the unclean things of her fornication, 5 and upon her forehead a name written, MYSTERY, BABYLON THE GREAT, THE MOTHER OF THE HARLOTS AND OF THE ABOMINATIONS**

OF THE EARTH. 6 And I saw the woman drunken with the blood of the saints, and with the blood of the martyrs of Jesus. The woman of chapter 12 represents the true church; the one of this chapter, the unfaithful church. Let us note some marks of her unfaithfulness. First, her association was evil—with the wild beast, by whom she was supported, instead of the Lamb. (See Rev. 14: 1.) Second, her attire was unfitting—purple and scarlet, like the dragon and the beast, instead of white. (Rev. 12: 1; 19: 8.) Third, her treasures were earthly—gold, pearls, precious stone. Her interest was not centered in things spiritual but temporal. Fourth, she was a harlot. This means that she had broken her marriage vow and was united with another. In the latter relationship unholy children were born—she was "the mother of harlots." In her sin she was shameless. How very different to the chaste virgin, espoused to Christ! And fifth, she was drunken with the blood of martyrs. This means that she was a persecuting power. She is a symbol of the unfaithful portion of Christ's church. **And when I saw her, I wondered with great wonder.** It was a mystery to John how the faithful wife—the true church—would prove untrue to her husband—the Lord Jesus.

"The two women are contrasted in every particular that is mentioned about them:

1. The one is pure as purity itself, 'made ready' and fit for heaven's unsullied holiness; the other foul as corruption could make her, fit only for the fires of destruction.

2. The one belongs to the Lamb, who loves her as the bridegroom loves the bride; the other is associated with the wild beast, and with the kings of the earth, who ultimately hate and destroy her.

3. The one is clothed with fine linen, and in another place is said to be clothed with the sun and crowned with a coronet of stars: that is, robed in divine righteousness and resplendent with heavenly glory; the other is attired in scarlet and gold, in jewels and pearls, gorgeous indeed, but with earthly splendor only.

4. The one is represented as a chaste virgin, espoused to Christ; the other is mother of harlots and abominations of the earth.

5. The one is persecuted, pressed hard by the dragon, driven into the wilderness, and well-nigh overwhelmed; the other is drunken with martyr's blood, and 'seated' on a beast which has received its power from the persecuting dragon.

6. The one sojourns in solitude in the wilderness; the other reigns 'in the wilderness' over people, and nations, and kindreds, and tongues.

7. The one goes in with the Lamb to the marriage supper, amid the glad hallelujahs; the other is stripped, insulted, torn, and destroyed by her guilty paramours.

8. We lose sight of the bride amid the effulgence of heavenly glory and joy, and of the harlot amid the gloom and darkness of the smoke that rose up forever and forever."

II. "A Scarlet-Colored Beast" (Verses 7-15)

7 And the angel said unto me, Wherefore didst thou wonder? I will tell thee the mystery of the woman, and of the beast that carried her, which hath the seven heads and the ten horns. 8 The beast that thou sawest was, and is not; and is about to come up out of the abyss, and to go into perdition. And they that dwell on the earth shall wonder, they whose names hath not been written in the book of life from the foundation of the world, when they behold the beast, how that he was, and is not, and shall come. 9 Here is the mind that hath wisdom. The seven heads are seven mountains, on which the woman sitteth: 10 and they are seven kings; the five are fallen, the one is, the other is not yet come; and when he cometh, he must continue a little while. 11 And the beast that was, and is not, is himself also an eighth, and is of the seven; and he goeth into perdition. 12 And the ten horns that thou sawest are ten kings, who have received no kingdom as yet; but they received authority as kings, with the beast, for one hour. 13 These have one mind, and they give their power and authority unto the beast. 14 These shall war against the Lamb, and the Lamb shall overcome them, for he is Lord of lords, and King of kings; and they also shall overcome that are with him, called and chosen and faithful. 15 And he saith unto me, The waters which thou sawest, where the harlot sitteth, are people, and multitudes, and nations, and tongues. Who is this beast? The same as "the waters," the "seven mountains," "people, and multitudes, and nations and tongues." The seven mountains, kings, or kingdoms mentioned in this paragraph are seven manifestations of the beast in successive eras of persecution suffered by God's people, including Egypt, Assyria, Babylon, Persia, Greece, and Rome ("one is" when John wrote.) At the fall of Rome, the seventh appeared. The eighth is the fiercest of all—the embodiment of all. The beast is "an eighth, and is of the seventh" in character. The beast is the spirit of worldliness. If we can identify him with the beast of chapter 13, the answer will be conclusive.

Chapter 13

(a) "Coming up out of the sea." Sea the source. (Verse 1.)

(b) "Ten horns and s e v e n heads." Horns are mentioned first b e c a u s e they appeared first, when he emerged from the sea. (Verse 1.)

(c) "On his horns ten diadems." (Verse 1.)

(d) "Upon his heads names of blasphemy." (Verse 1.)

(e) Vicegerent of the dragon. Warred against saints. (Verses 2, 7.)

(f) Was raised from the dead. (Verse 3.)

(g) World wondered after him. (Verse 3.)

Chapter 17

(a) "About to come out of the abyss." (Verse 8.) The abyss his temporary abode. Comes out of the sea, lives, dies, goes into abyss, rises from dead.

(b) "Seven h e a d s and ten horns." He is seen in the wilderness; hence the order of nature is preserved. (Verse 3.)

(c) No diadems are mentioned. The ten kings have received no kingdom as yet. (Verse 12.)

(d) "Full of names of blasphemy." John saw the entire beast. (Verse 3.)

(e) Engaged in same work. (Verse 14.)

(f) Raised f r o m the dead. (Verse 8.)

(g) W o r l d wondered a f t e r him. (Verse 8.)

III. The Relation of the Two (Verses 16-18)

16 **And the ten horns,** indicating plentitude of power or influence, **which thou sawest, and the beast, these shall hate the harlot, and shall make her desolate and naked, and shall eat her flesh, and shall burn her utterly with fire.** 17 **For God did put in their hearts to do his mind, and to come to one mind, and to give their kingdom unto the beast, until the words of God should be accomplished.** 18 **And the woman whom thou sawest is the great city, which reigneth over the kings of the earth.** Between the beast (the spirit of worldliness) and the harlot (the false church) we see a twofold relationship. First, partnership. The beast supported the woman and was ruled by her. (See verses 3, 18.) When the church sinks in her moral and spiritual life to the level of the world, the world patronizes her, listens to her counsel. We recall that the Roman world supported the Jewish church in the execution of our Lord. Second, enmity. Ere long the world loses its respect for the apostate, the harlot-church. When the church sinks to the level of the world, the world eventually turns and rends her. After the crucifixion of Jesus, the Roman state turned against the Jewish church

and all but destroyed her. For the harlot, men—even evil men—have no respect. They hate her. They abuse her. They devour her.

From This Chapter Learn:

1. That there are two churches—the true and the false. The true church is represented by the woman of chapter 12, the false by the woman of chapter 17.

2. That if our association is with the Christ—if he is the center of our affection and the Lord of our life—we are members of the true church.

3. That if our association is with the beast (the spirit of worldliness)—if he is the center of our affection and the lord of our life —we are members of the false church.

4. That the false church is a harlot. She has forsaken the Lord Jesus, her true husband, and is joined unto a beast—this present evil world. The children now born to her are unholy. From the apostate church radiates an unholy influence.

5. That when the Christian turns to the world, he is at first honored by the world. Eventually, however, the world will turn and devour the unfaithful Christian. The world has no respect for the harlot-church.

Memory Selection

"These shall war against the Lamb, and the Lamb shall overcome them, for he is Lord of lords, and King of kings; and they also shall overcome that are with him, called and chosen and faithful." (Verse 14.)

Daily Readings

Monday: The Radiant Woman. (Rev. 12: 1-17.)
Tuesday: The Beast of the Land. (Rev. 13: 1-10.)
Wednesday: The Ten Kingdoms. (Dan. 7: 1-28.)
Thursday: "Let Us Fear Therefore." (Heb. 4: 1-16.)
Friday: "They Crucify the Son of God Afresh." (Heb. 4: 1-16.)
Saturday: Turning Back. (2 Pet. 2: 1-22.)

For Class Discussion

1. Of what is "Babylon the Great" a symbol? Is it the same as the wicked woman of this chapter?

2. Describe the woman—her association, her attire, her treasures. What does she represent? Explain verse 6.

3. Draw a contrast between the woman of chapter 12 and the woman of chapter 17.

4. Identify the beast that supported the woman. Show that the beast of chapter 17 is the same as the beast of chapter 13. Show that the beast represents the spirit of worldliness in its various manifestations.

5. Discuss the relation of the woman and the beast, the corrupt church and the world. When the church, or a Christian, compromises with the world, what does the world eventually turn and do?

6. What practical points are suggested in this chapter? Quote the memory selection.

"FALLEN, FALLEN IS BABYLON"

Text: Rev. 18: 1-24   **Lesson XXII**

In the preceding chapter "Babylon the Great" was described, its sinful nature revealed. In the chapter we now open, so dramatic in appeal, we have a prophecy of her fall. Three prominent divisions are obvious, namely: The announcement of her fall; the emotional reaction to her fall; and the finality of her fall.

I. The Announcement of Her Fall (Verses 1-8)

1 **After these things I saw another angel coming down out of heaven, having great authority; and the earth was lighted with his glory.** "The description of this angel is proportionate to the importance of his message." (Milligan.) 2 **And he cried with a mighty voice, saying, Fallen, fallen is Babylon the great, and is become a habitation of demons, and a hold** (prison) **of every unclean spirit, and a hold of every unclean and hateful bird.** A most tragic disaster of by-gone days, the destruction of ancient Babylon, is a type of the fall of the apostate church. (Read Isa. 13: 19-22.) 3 **For by the wine of the wrath of her fornication all the nations are fallen.** This is a forceful reminder of the hurtful influence of false Christianity. **And the kings of the earth committed fornication with her, and the merchants of the earth waxed rich by the power of her wantonness.** Very graphically does this verse point out the cause of her fall— she is carnally minded.

4 **And I heard another voice from heaven, saying, Come forth, my people, out of her, that he have no fellowship with her sins, and that ye receive not of her plagues: 5 for her sins have reached even unto heaven, and God hath remembered her iniquities.** This is a call

to the true church. The exodus here demanded is not bodily, but spiritual; not necessarily from places, but from principles; not from persons, but from characters; from participation in sin. (Read 2 Cor. 6: 14-18.) He who partakes of her sins must also partake of her plagues. **6 Render unto her even as she rendered, and double unto her the double according to her works: in the cup which she mingled, mingle unto her double.** 7 **How much soever she glorified herself, and waxed wanton, so much give her of torment and mourning.** God calls upon the executioners of his wrath to inflict the penalty. (See Rev. 17: 16, 17.) In wickedness she is double-stained, and her punishment is according to her deeds. She has drunk the strained wine; now she must drink the bitter dregs. She has sown wantonness; now she must reap "torment and mourning." **For she saith in her heart, I sit a queen, and am no widow, and shall in no wise see mourning.** Instead of mourning in the absence of the Bridegroom, she sits in ease, refusing to be called a widow. She is content with the wild-beast—the spirit of carnality. 8 **Therefore in one day shall her plagues come, death, and mourning, and famine; she shall be utterly burned with fire; for strong is the Lord God who judged her.** Though apostasy may be long in the making, the punishment will be sudden. "In one day" will come the three-fold plague—death, mourning, and famine.

II. Emotional Reactions to Her Fall (Verses 9-20)

The fall of Babylon excites the emotions of all mankind—of evil men, also of righteous men. But their emotions are not the same. While evil men mourn over her fall, the righteous rejoice.

1. Mourning

In the verses that follow, we have a three-fold dirge—the dirge of kings, the dirge of merchants, and the dirge of mariners.

9 **And the kings of the earth, who committed fornication and lived wantonly with her, shall weep and wail over her, when they look upon the smoke of her burning, 10 standing afar off for the fear of her torment, saying, Woe, woe, the great city, Babylon, the strong city! for in one hour is thy judgment come.** They were greatly saddened and surprised by the swift overthrow of power and reverse of fortune.

11 **And the merchants of the earth weep and mourn over her, for no man buyeth her merchandise any more; 12 merchants of gold, and silver, and precious stone, and pearls, and the linen, and purple, and silk, and scarlet.** Such was the attire of the harlot, as we

learned in chapter 17. **And all thyine wood, and every vessel of ivory, and every vessel made of most precious wood, and of brass, and iron, and marble; 13 and cinnamon, and spice, and incense, and ointment, and frankincense, and wine, and oil, and fine flour, and wheat, and cattle, and sheep; and merchandise of horses and chariots and slaves; and souls** (lives) **of men. 14 And the fruits which thy soul lusted after are gone from thee, and all things that were dainty and sumptuous are perished from thee, and men shall find them no more at all.** This verse contains a direct appeal to Babylon. **15 The merchants of these things, who were made rich by her, shall stand afar off for the fear of her torment, weeping and mourning; 16 saying, Woe, woe, the great city, she that was arrayed in fine linen and purple and scarlet, and decked with gold and precious stone and pearl; 17 for in one hour so great riches is made desolate.** Thus, the merchants mourn the loss of profitable market.

And every shipmaster, and every one that saileth any whither, and mariners, and as many as gain their living by sea, stood afar off, 18 and cried out as they looked upon the smoke of her burning, saying, What city is like the great city? 19 And they cast dust on their heads, and cried, weeping and mourning, saying, Woe, woe, the great city, wherein all that had ships in the sea were made rich by reason of her costliness! for in one hour is she made desolate. Thus, the mariners mourn the blow inflicted on shipping trade.

All who mourn her fate point out the fact that her destruction is swift and sudden—"in one hour." The apostle John sees not a decline but collapse. Emphasis is laid on the fact that she is burned. According to Moses' law (Lev. 21: 9), burning appears to have been the form of punishment for fornication only in case of a priest's daughter—another indication that Babylon is a wicked religious power.

2. Rejoicing

20 Rejoice over her, thou heaven, and ye saints, and ye apostles, and ye prophets; for God hath judged your judgment on her. Three classes of worldly men—kings, merchants, and mariners—lament Babylon's fall; three classes of righteous men—saints, apostles and prophets—are called upon to rejoice over her fall. While those who have vested interested in the maintenance of Babylon howl in anguish at the fall of falsehood, there are others transported with rapture when they see her descending to her doom. Worldly men and righteous men neither mourn nor rejoice over the same things. This is true because they have different points of interest, of affection.

III. The Finality· of Her Fall (Verses 21-24)

21 **And a strong angel took up a stone as it were a great millstone and cast it into the sea, saying, Thus with a mighty fall shall Babylon, the great city, be cast down, and shall be found no more at all. 22 And the voice of harpers and minstrels and flute-players and trumpeters shall be heard no more at all in thee; and no craftsman, of whatsoever craft, shall be found any more at all in thee; and the voice of a mill shall be heard no more at all in thee; 23 and the light of a lamp shall shine no more at all in thee; and the voice of the bridegroom and of the bride shall be heard no more at all in thee: for thy merchants were the princes of the earth; for with thy sorcery were all the nations deceived.** Six times over does the expression "no more" appear in this paragraph, and each time concerning the same solemn fact—the fall of "Babylon the Great." The city is to be "no more," her music "no more," her trade "no more," her food supplies "no more," her lamp-lit feasts "no more," and her marriage "no more." The fall of the city is symbolized by the dramatic action of "a strong angel," lifting aloft a huge and ponderous millstone and then hurling it, with all his might, into the depth of the sea. There, buried out of sight, it shall never again be seen. At one moment we see the city in her brightness, her gaiety, her activity. All that can please the eye is seen, all that can please the ear is heard. The next moment the proud city sinks into eternal oblivion, and all is silence, desolation and ruin. The last verse of the chapter opens up her inner life and reveals a cause of her destruction—the cruelty of oppression and persecution.

From This Chapter Learn:

1. That the departure from God is a tragic fall. This fall is not physical, but moral and spiritual in nature. It is a fall from truth to error, from virtue to vice, from love to hatred, from freedom to slavery, from joy to sorrow, from sunshine to midnight darkness, from the Savior to Satan.

2. That the true church within the false is called out. This means that we are not to partake of false doctrine or false practice. He who becomes a partaker of the sins of the false church, will become a partaker of her punishment.

3. That the unfaithful soul is doomed to desolation, "a habitation of demons, and a hold of every unclean spirit, and a hold of every unclean and hateful bird." Those who refuse "to have God in their knowledge," will be given "up unto a reprobate mind." (Rom. 1: 28-32.)

4. That the fall of Babylon, the corrupt church, is at once the occasion of both sorrow and joy—sorrow on the part of the worldly minded, joy on the part of the heavenly minded.

5. That the fall of Babylon is great for three reasons: because of the suddenness of it—the suddenness of a millstone cast into the sea; because of the completeness of it—like a millstone, it is sunk bodily into the depths of the sea; because of the finality of it—like a millstone in the sea, never to rise again.

Memory Selection

"Come forth, my people, out of her, that ye have no fellowship with her sins, and that ye receive not of her plagues." (Verse 4.)

Daily Readings
Monday: "The Burden of Babylon." (Isa. 13: 1-22.)
Tuesday: A Day of Desolation. (Isa. 34: 1-17.)
Wednesday: The Fall of Tyre. (Ezek. 26: 1-21.)
Thursday: The Lament over Tyre. (Ezek. 27: 1-36.)
Friday: "Come Ye Out." (2 Cor. 6: 1-18.)
Saturday: "Great Was the Fall Thereof." (Matt. 7: 24-27.)

For Class Discussion
1. Discuss briefly the content of chapter 17. State the subject of the lesson before us and show its connection with chapter 17.

2. In verses 1-3, what solemn announcement is made? by whom was it made? What is the Babylon of Revelation?

3. In verses 4-8 what call is given to God's true people? What is the meaning of this call? In the same verses, what reason is given for Babylon's fall?

4. Who mourns the fall of Babylon? why? Who rejoices over her fall? why? Over what things do the wicked mourn? Over what things do the righteous rejoice?

5. Discuss the completeness of her fall, as dramatized in verses 21-24. Point out three reasons why the fall of Babylon is a great fall.

6. What practical lessons do we glean from the assignment? Quote the memory selection.

PART VII

The Consummation
(Rev. 19: 1-22: 21)

THE VICTORY OF THE LAMB

Text: Rev. 19: 1-21   **Lesson XXIII**

The corrupt church, represented by Babylon, having been destroyed, the marriage supper of the lamb with the glorified church is announced. Before the grand event can take place, the other enemies of Christ and his kingdom must be destroyed. In chapters 19 and 20 come visions of the final victory of the Lamb over these enemies. In chapter 19 we have "A Great Voice," A Great Warrior, "A Great Supper," and A Great Victory.

I. "A Great Voice" (Verses 1-10)

Over the fall of Babylon, the world has poured out its lamentations. (Rev. 18: 9-20.) How very different are the emotions of the forces of righteousness! They rejoice greatly. The chapter opens with the "Hallelujah Chorus."

1 **After these things I heard as it were a great voice of a great multitude in heaven, saying, Hallelujah,** meaning, "Praise ye Jehovah." Though frequently found in the Psalms, the word appears only here in the New Testament. It is chiefly used in connection with the punishment of the wicked. **Salvation, and glory, and power, belong to our God: 2 for true and righteous are his judgments; for he hath judged the great harlot (the false church), her that corrupted the earth with her fornications, and he hath avenged the blood of her servants at her hands.**

3 **And a second time they say, Hallelujah. And,** in the meantime, **her smoke goeth up for ever and ever. 4 And the four and twenty elders and the four living creatures fell down and worshipped God that sitteth on the throne, saying, Amen ("So be it"), Hallelujah. 5 And a voice came forth from the throne, saying, Give praise to our God, all ye his servants, ye that fear him, the small and the great.** The voice from the throne called for renewed praise and the response was immediate.

6 **And I heard as it were the voice of a great multitude, and as the voice of many waters, and as the voice of mighty thunders, saying, Hallelujah: for the Lord our God, the Almighty reigneth. 7 Let us rejoice and be exceeding glad, and let us give the glory**

unto him: for the marriage of the Lamb is come, and his wife (the true church) hath made herself ready. This she did by adorning herself with works of righteousness, as pointed out in the next verse. 8 And it was given unto her that she should array herself in fine linen, bright and pure: for the fine linen is the righteous acts of the saints. "Happiness and virtue reach upon each other—the best are not only the happiest, but the happiest are usually the best." (Lytton.)

From whom came this rejoicing? From a mighty host in heaven. From "the four and twenty elders," representatives of the redeemed church. From "the four living creatures," angels of a very high order. From God's servants, "the small and the great." "As the voice of many waters," their voice was continuous. "As the voice of mighty thunders," it was strong and distinct.

What was the ground of their joy? First, the manifestations of God's power. Unto him belong "salvation, and glory, and power." He is able to lift all who love him, to cast down the proud and haughty, even mighty Babylon. Second, the manifestation of God's justice: for he has "judged" and "avenged." Third, the manifestation of God's mercy. Upon those ready to perish, he has bestowed salvation; he has adorned them with loveliness—"made them fair, though he found them foul." And fourth, the manifestation of the Lord's faithfulness. He keeps inviolate his marriage vow. He is true to his bride for whom he will come and claim as his own. The tie between Christ and the true church shall never be broken; it will outlive the "wreck of matter, and the crash of worlds."

II. The Great Warrier (Verses 11-16)

11 And I saw the heaven opened; and behold, a white horse, and he that sat thereon called Faithful and True; and in righteousness he doth judge and make war. 12 And his eyes are a flame of fire, and upon his head are many diadems; and he hath a name written which no one knoweth but he himself. 13 And he is arrayed in a garment sprinkled with blood: and his name is called The Word of God. 14 And the armies which are in heaven followed him upon white horses, clothed in fine linen, white and pure. 15 And out of his mouth proceedeth a sharp sword, that with it he should smite the nations: and he shall rule them with a rod of iron: and he treadeth the winepress of the fierceness of the wrath of God, the Almighty. 16 And he hath on his garments and on his thigh a name written, KING OF KINGS, AND LORD OF LORDS. Now comes the great leader and his heavenly host. Until his final triumph, the marriage

supper cannot take place. He has already conquered—he now comes forth to inflict the punishment. (See 2 Thess. 1: 7-10.) Concerning the great warrior, let us make some inquiries.

Who is he, and what is his name? First, he is "called Faithful and True." His name is an index to his character. He is an embodiment of fidelity, of all that is true. Second, "he hath a name written which no one knoweth but he himself." Some aspects of his nature are known to us, else we could not love him or follow him. But there are depths of his nature that we cannot fathom. "No one knoweth the Son but the Father." Third, "his name is called The Word of God." He is the expression of God's thoughts, of God's will, of God's personality. And fourth, he is "King of kings, and Lord of lords." This indicates his dignity, his authority. (See Matt. 28: 18.)

And what are his qualities? How shall we describe him? First, he appears on "a white horse." This means that his cause is righteous. "In righteousness he doth judge and make war." Second, "his eyes are a flame of fire." He is omniscient. Nothing, good or evil, escapes his notice. Third, "upon his head are many diadems." Doubtless, this is an allusion to the ancient custom of a conquering king wearing the diadems of the vanquished. As earthly crowns fall from kingly brows, he to whom the nations belong shall bear their glory. In all places his righteous will shall prevail. Fourth, "he is arrayed in a garment sprinkled with blood"—the blood of foes he has conquered. The blood is not literal, but symbolic, indicating the completeness of his victory. And fifth, "out of his mouth, preceedeth a sharp sword," which is his word—the power by which he saves the obedient and subdues the disobedient.

III. "A Great Supper" (Verses 17, 18)

17 **And I saw an angel standing in the sun,** "a place befitting his glory, and also whence he can appropriately issue his summons," **and he cried with a loud voice, saying to all the birds that fly in mid heaven, Come and be gathered together unto the great supper of God;** 18 **that ye may eat the flesh of kings, and the flesh of captains, and the flesh of mighty men, and the flesh of horses and of them that sit thereon, and the flesh of all men, both free and bond, and small and great.** The birds "that fly in mid heaven" (vultures and eagles) are invited to glut themselves on the enemies of Christ. (See Ezek. 39: 17-20.) This is a contrast and travesty of the marriage supper of the Lamb. While saints are partaking of the marriage supper, the wicked are themselves food for obscene birds. In the

last day, there shall be two great suppers. Either we shall have the joy of eating with the Lamb, or we shall supply refreshment to ravenous birds.

IV. A Great Victory (Verses 19-21)

19 And I saw the beast, and the kings of the earth, and their armies, gathered together to make war against him that sat upon the horse, and against his army. 20 And the beast was taken, and with him the false prophet that wrought the signs in his sight, wherewith he deceived them that had received the mark of the beast and them that worshipped his image: they two were cast alive into the lake of fire that burneth with brimstone: 21 and the rest were killed with the sword of him that sat upon the horse, even the sword which came forth out of his mouth: and all the birds were filled with their flesh. In this paragraph we have the final overthrow of the beast, the false prophet and their followers. The forces of evil are assembled, but no battle is seen. They fall by a sudden stroke of the Lamb. They are cast "alive into the lake of fire." (See Rev. 21: 8.) Verse 21 tells of a remnant not numbered with the beast and the prophet.

From This Chapter Learn:

1. That the overthrow of Babylon (false religion), will be the occasion of great rejoicing on the part of God's people. While "her smoke goeth up," they shall sing in unison the grand "Hallelujah Chorus."

2. That the appearance of the great Warrior on "a white horse" in the history of mankind began to turn the tide of the forces of evil. When the gospel began to be preached, sin began to recede: for the gospel "is the power of God."

3. That Christ is reigning. He is reigning through the power of his word. He is reigning in every heart that will yield to the gospel. When he comes in the cloud of his glory, the final stroke will be delivered.

Memory Selection

"And it was given unto her that she should array herself in fine linen, bright and pure: for the fine linen is the righteous acts of the saints." (Verse 8.)

Daily Readings

Monday: "Praise Ye Jehovah." (Psa. 135: 1-21.)
Tuesday: The Burning of Babylon. (Rev. 18: 1-24.)
Wednesday: The Marriage Between the Lord and His People. (Isa. 54: 1-8; Hosea 2: 19ff; Ezek. 16: 7ff; Eph. 5: 1-33.)
Thursday: The Christ of Glory. (Rev. 1: 12-18.)
Friday: The Enemies of Christ.—The Dragon. (Rev. 12: 1-17.)
Saturday: The Enemies of Christ.—The Two Beasts. (Rev. 13: 1-18.) 1-18.)

For Class Discussion

1. Review briefly the lesson of chaper 18. What is the subject of the lesson of the day?

2. When Babylon fell, what were the emotions of the forces of evil? of the forces of righteousness? In what way did the emotions of God's people find expression? Discuss.

3. In verses 11-16, what great Warrior appeared? What was his mission? Who is he, and what are his names? What is the significance of each name? What are his qualities? How shall we describe him?

4. Give a word-picture of "a great supper" as given in verses 17 and 18. What is the significance of it?

5. What can you say of the great victory, as depicted in verses 19-21? What enemies were overthrown?

THE DRAGON'S DOOM

Text: Rev. 20: 1-15   **Lesson XXIV**

In chapters 12 and 13 we were introduced to the three great enemies of the church, namely: "A great red dragon" (the devil), the beast of the sea (the world), and the beast of the land (false religion). In chapters 18 and 19 we saw the ultimate defeat of the last two. The defeat of the dragon is reserved for chapter 20. The overthrow of the dragon, not the millennial reign, is the theme of this chapter. In an effort to explain this scripture portion, let us not misplace the emphasis or exalt a detail to a place of prime importance. We shall study the binding of the dragon, the millenial reign, the dragon's doom, and the final judgment.

I. The Dragon Bound (Verses 1-3)

1 **And I saw an angel coming down out of heaven, having the key to the abyss and a great chain in his hand.** At the close of the last chapter, we were carried forward to the end of time. We

now return to the dawn of the Christian era, when the Sun of Righteousness arose with healing in his beams. 2 **And he laid hold on the dragon, the old serpent, which is the Devil and Satan, and bound him for a thousand years, 3 and cast him into the abyss, and shut it, and sealed it over that he should deceive the nations no more, until the thousand years should be finished: after this he must be loosed for a little time.** In these verses we have a representation in significant imagry of the restraint that is placed upon evil by divine power. First, note the restraining "angel," a representative of the Savior. Second, the one restrained, "the dragon, the old serpent"—the destroyer, the enemy of all righteousness. The place of the confinement is the "abyss," the present abode of the devil and his angels, whence they direct their operations in opposition to God. The place of their final punishment is "the lake of fire." (Verse 10.) Third, the instrument, "a great chain." This is the chain of gospel truth, God's power to save. (Rom. 1: 16.) What else could it be? The work of binding the dragon began when Jesus began to triumph over him. (Read Matt. 4: 1-11; 12: 29; Luke 10: 17, 18; John 12: 31, 32; 16: 7-11, 33; Matt. 28: 1-10; Acts 2.) The heavenly restrains the earthly, even holds back the satanic. Fourth, the duration of the restraint is "a thousand years," a considerable period of time. In keeping with the nature of the context, we shall make no effort to literalize this expression. We do not give a literal interpretation to the "key," to the "chain," and to other expressions of this chapter. Why should we insist on a literal interpretation of "a thousand years"?

II. The Millennial Reign (Verses 4-6)

4 **And I saw thrones, and they sat upon them, and judgment was given unto them: and I saw the souls** (not bodies) **of them that had been beheaded for the testimony of Jesus, and for the word of God, and such as worshipped not the beast, neither his image, and received not the mark upon their forehead and upon their hand; and they lived and reigned with Christ a thousand years.** The binding of the dragon is naturally followed by a period of spiritual progress when the followers of Christ are highly exalted. The reference to the martyrs was made in order to encourage the faithful in their trials ·and tribulations. "You Christians sit upon thrones and reign with Christ; yea, even those who suffered shameful deaths shared this perfect safety and exaltation, though to the eyes of the world they were so afflicted and degraded." Many of the later Jews expected the Messianic kingdom to continue for a thousand years. Obviously, John made use of the expectation,

but it does not follow that he meant for it to be understood literally. **5 The rest of the dead lived not until the thousand years should be finished.** These were sinners who will not experience a resurrection of any kind until the end of time, when they shall have part in the general resurrection. (Verses 12 and 13.) **This is the first resurrection,** i.e., the exhaltation and reign with Christ during the thousand years. The New Testament speaks of two resurrections, namely, the resurrection of the body from the literal tomb, and the resurrection of the soul from the tomb of sin. (Read John 5: 25-29.) The resurrection of the body will take place "in the last day" (John 5: 44), at the descent of the Lord (1 Thess. 4: 16), at the end of the Christian era (1 Cor. 15: 20-24). But the resurrection of the soul from the tomb of sin is taking place in the present, the gospel dispensation. Jesus said, "The hour cometh, and now is, when the dead shall hear the voice of the Son of God; and they that hear shall live." The apostle Paul was speaking of the same resurrection —a spiritual awakening—when he wrote to the Ephesians: "You did he make. alive, when ye were dead through your trespasses and sins . . . and raised us up with him, and made us to sit with him in heavenly places in Christ Jesus." (Eph, 2.) This is a resurrection! Being the first one that the saints at Ephesus had experienced, it must have been "the first resurrection." Verily, the first is "first"! **6 Blessed and holy is he that hath part in the first resurrection: over these the second death hath no power; but they shall be priests of God and of Christ, and shall reign with him a thousand years.** To those who are raised with Christ, and walk with Christ (Rom. 6: 1-4) comes a three-fold blessedness: They are immune from the second death (Rev. 21: 8); they enjoy priestly privileges—access to the throne of graces; they exercise kingly power—they rule by their influence (Matt. 5: 14).

III. The Dragon's Doom (Verses 7-10)

7 And when the thousand years are finished, Satan shall be loosed out of his prison, 8 and shall come forth to deceive the nations which are in the four corners of the earth, Gog and Magog. John took these names (Ezek. 38: 2) to be symbolical of the enemies of God's people. **To gather them together to the war: the number of whom is as the sand of the sea. 9 And they went up over the breadth of the earth, and compassed the camp of the saints about, and the beloved city,** spiritual Jerusalem or the church. To the happy period described in the preceding paragraph there comes a temporary relapse. When the final judgment is at hand, the powers of evil will again assemble and gather force. (Read 1 Tim. 4:

1ff; 2 Tim. 3: 13; 2 Pet. 3: 3ff.) **And fire came down out of heaven, and devoured them. 10 And the devil that deceived them was cast into the lake of fire and brimstone, where are also the beast and the false prophet; and they shall be tormented day and night forever and ever.** The relapse, we note, is only temporary—"for a little time"—and issues in the final destruction of the dragon and his followers. His fellow-sufferers are the "beast" (the worldly or ir-religious people) and the "false prophet" (the corrupt church).

IV. The Final Judgment (Verses 11-15)

11 And I saw a great white throne, and him that sat upon it, from whose face the earth and heaven fled away; and there was found no place for them. 12 And I saw the dead, the great and the small, standing before the throne; and books were opened; and another book was opened, which is the book of life: and the dead were judged out of the things which were written in the books, according to their works. 13 And the sea gave up the dead that were in it; and death and Hades gave up the dead that were in them: and they were judged every man according to their works. 14 And death and Hades were cast into the lake of fire. This is the second death, even the lake of fire. 15 And if any was not found written in the book of life, he was cast into the lake of fire. The scenes of history are approaching completion. Very definitely they present the characteristics of the end of the world and the finality in the affairs of men. In this paragraph we have a word picture of the last judgment. We note: First, the authority of it—it is "a great throne." The decisions which issue therefrom are immutable. The Judge has "all authority" in heaven and on earth. - Second, the sanctity of it—it is a "white throne." White is a symbol of purity, of righteousness. "We know that the judgment of God is according to truth." Third, the dread terribleness of it. This is indicated in the statement that the "earth and heaven fled away" from "the face" of the Judge. Fourth, the universality of it. John saw "the dead, the great and the small, standing before the throne." From the sea, from death and Hades they come. The judgment is upon "the dead," indicating that the ultimate issues of human society have come. Fifth, the individuality of it—"they were judged every man." There was no escape in the vastness of the multitude. (See Rom. 14: 12.) Sixth, the justice of it. Not according to rank, or race, or riches, or social standing, or political power, but "according to their works" were men judged. "In the books" the "works" are recorded. And seventh, the finality of it. "If any was not found written in the book of life (God's family record), he was cast into the lake of fire." That the dramatic scene represents the termination of the present order of things is clearly indicated by the destruction of death and Hades; the present, the temporary, is swallowed up in the final. Only one side of judgment is depicted—that of the wicked. They have as their fellow sufferers the beast, the false prophet, and the dragon.

From This Chapter Learn:

1. That, when Jesus came, men were in the clutches of sin, bound by the dragon.

2. That Jesus, by means of his life and teaching, especially by his victory over death, began to bind the dragon—to limit his unholy power. The one who had bound men was bound by the Friend of men. In the light of the gospel, Satan can have no power at all except that which men of their own accord grant him.

3. That the reign of the dragon ends where the reign of Christ begins. This is true from a historical viewpoint; it is true in the life of an individual. For every man who loves the Lord supremely, dragon is bound.

4. That all who believe the gospel, obey the gospel and follow its holy precepts are raised from the tomb of sin. They experience "the first resurrection." There is no resurrection for them before this.

5. That the day of final accounts is approaching. From this we cannot turn back. From this there is no escape.

Memory Selection

"And if any was not found written in the book of life, he was cast into the lake of fire." (Verse 15.)

Daily Readings

Monday: The Fall of Man. (Gen. 3: 1-24.)
Tuesday: God With Us. (Matt. 2: 18-25.)
Wednesday: Victory Over Temptation. (Luke 4: 1-13.)
Thursday: Victory Over Demons. (Mark 3: 1-35; 5: 1-20.)
Friday: Victory Over Sorrow. (Matt. 26: 36-46.)
Saturday: Victory 'Over Death. (Matt. 28: 1-10.)

For Class Discussion

1. What is the lesson subject?
2. Name the three enemies of the church, to whom we were introduced in chapters 12 and 13. In chapters 18 and 19, the fall of what two enemies of the church was depicted? In chapter 20, the fall of what great enemy of the church is depicted?
3. Discuss the binding of the dragon, as told in verses 1-3. What is the power that binds him?
4. What follows the binding of the dragon, as depicted in verses 4-6?
5. When did the reign of Christ begin in history? When does it begin in the life of an individual?
6. What is "the first resurrection"? What can you say of the blessedness of it?
7. Discuss the dragon's doom, as told in verses 7-10.
8. Describe the final judgment, as told in verses 11-15.
9. What practical lessons have you learned from the lesson. Quote the memory selection.

THE NEW JERUSALEM

Text: Rev. 21: 1-22: 5   **Lesson XXV**

The storm clouds have disappeared never to return and the sky is clear. The foes of God's people have been conquered and consigned to their doom. The judgment is over and the state of things, as we now know it, has passed away. The beloved John, still an exile on Patmos, sees in a vision another dwelling place, bright and beautiful, in which the redeemed live forever. This place is called the "new Jerusalem." In the first part of our assignment, we see the city descending. In the last part we have a more minute description of the city—of its exterior, then of its interior.

I. The City Descending (Verses 1-8)

1 **And I saw a new heaven and a new earth: for the first heaven and the first earth are passed away; and the sea is no more.** Here we have a new order or environment characterized by two things. First, by righteousness. A change of the heaven and earth symbolizes a spiritual change. (See 2 Pet. 3: 5-13.) Second, by contentment. The sea, forever in motion, is a type of perpetual unrest, of anxiety. But the sea of unrest, the sea of anxiety "is no more." The peace that passes understanding prevails. 2 **And I saw the holy city, new Jerusalem, coming down out of heaven from God, made ready as a bride adorned for her husband. 3 And I heard a**

great voice out of heaven saying, Behold, the tabernacle of God is with men, and he shall dwell with them, and they shall be his peoples, and God himself shall be with them, and be their God: 4 and he shall wipe away every tear from their eyes; and death shall be no more; neither shall there be mourning, nor crying, nor pain, any more: the first things are passed away. New Jerusalem represents God's people. Not only shall there be a new environment, but also a new people—old people with new bodies fitted for the new environment. Their character and privileges are described. First, they are a heavenly people—a heavenly minded people. The city came down "out of heaven from God." Unlike the city of Babylon, which was earthly. Second, they are attired with the beauty of holiness—"made ready as a bride adorned for her husband." (See Rev. 19: 8.) Unlike the harlot, who was adorned with earthly splendor. (See Rev. 17: 4, 5.) And third, they are on intimate terms with God the Father. They belong to him; he belongs to them. He dwells among them; and removes sorrow and death and pain. 5 **And he that sitteth on the throne said, Behold, I make all things new. And he said, Write: for these words are faithful and true.** Old t h i n g s worthy to live, shall be made new. Paradise, wrecked by the fall, shall be restored, yea, more than restored! These things are wrought by him who "sitteth on the throne," whose words are "faithful and true." 6 **And he said unto me, They are come to pass. I am the Alpha and the Omega, the beginning and the end. I will give unto him that is athirst of the fountain of the water of life freely. 7 He that overcometh shall inherit these things; and I will be his God, and he shall be my son.** Lest the saints should despair of attaining the precious promises enumerated, a word of encouragement is added by "the Alpha and the Omega," who has power to fulfill the promises. The thirsty may drink freely from the fountain—every longing of the righteous soul will find complete satisfaction. The overcomer shall inherit these new things and walk with God as son with father. 8 **But for the fearful, and unbelieving, and abominable, and murderers, and fornicators, and sorcerers, and idolators, and all liars, their part shall be in the lake that burneth with fire and brimstone; which is the second death.** They had no part in the first (the spiritual) resurrection (Rev. 20: 6); therefore, they shall not inherit the precious promises, but the second death.

II. The City—Its Exterior (Verses 9-21)

9 **And there came one of the seven angels who had the seven bowls, who were laden with the seven last plagues.** (Rev. 17: 1);

and he spake with me, saying, Come hither, I will show thee the bride, the wife of the Lamb. 10 And he carried me away in the Spirit to a mountain great and high, where a clear vision might be obtained, and showed me the holy city, Jerusalem, coming down out of heaven from God, 11 having the glory of God. In the wilderness John had seen the harlot (Rev. 17: 1-3), the corrupt church. From a mountain "great and high," he saw the bride of Christ, the celestial city, the true church in her glory. Her light (luminary) was like unto a stone most precious, as it were a jasper stone, clear as crystal: 12 having a wall great and high; having twelve gates, and at the twelve gates twelve angels; and names written thereon, which are the names of the twelve tribes of the children of Israel: 13 and on the east were three gates; and on the north three gates; and on the south three gates; and on the west three gates. When the twelve tribes of Israel encamped in the wilderness, three tribes faced the east, three faced the north, three faced the south, and three faced the west. (See Num. 2; Ezek. 48.) 14 And the wall of the city had twelve foundations, and on them twelve names of the twelve apostles of the Lamb. 15 And he that spake with me had for a measure a golden reed to measure the city, and the gates thereof, and the wall thereof. 16 And the city lieth foursquare, and the length thereof is as great as the breadth: and he measured the city with a reed, twelve thousand furlongs: the length and the breadth and the height thereof are equal. 17 And he measured the wall thereof, a hundred and forty and four cubits, according to the measure of a man, that is, of an angel. 18 And the building of the wall thereof was jasper: and the city was pure gold, like unto pure glass. 19 The foundations of the wall of the city were adorned with all manner of precious stones. The first foundation was jasper; the second, sapphire; the third, chalcedony; the fourth, emerald; 20 the fifth, sardonyx; the sixth, sardis; the seventh, chrysolite; the eighth, beryl; the ninth, topaz; the tenth, chrysoprase; the eleventh, jacinth; the twelfth, amethyst. 21 And the twelve gates were twelve pearls; each one of the s e v e r a l gates was of one pearl: and the street of the city was pure gold, as it were transparent glass. This is an exterior description of the holy city. M a r v e l o u s is the apostle's language, symbolizing all that is pure and lovely. Note the following. First, the brightness of it. (Verse 11.) God is there and the city beams with the light of his glory. (See Rev. 12: 1; 19: 8.) Second, the security of it. The wall of it is "great and high." No enemy can penetrate its thickness or scale the height. The old serpent, who found his way into Eden, is forever excluded. Third, the accessibility of it. It has twelve gates, three facing each direction—the east, the north, the south, and the west. The godly of every nation may enter. (See Matt. 8: 11.) But the guardian angels at the gates exclude the unclean. (See Gen. 3: 24.) Fourth, the permanence of it. It is built upon "twelve foundations," or the eternal truth taught by the apostles of the Lamb. Truth shall never change or perish. Fifth, the perfection of it. It is a perfect cube, a well-proportioned city (Verses 15-17.) There are no disproportions or inequalities or injustices about it. The shape is doubtless typical of that which is complete or symmetrical. The city is spacious enough for all of God's children, whose number is twelve. (Here, twelve is multiplied one thousand, heaven's number.) And sixth, the splendor of the city. (Verses 18-21.) In the foundations, in its gates and in its streets radiant beauty is found. "How beautiful heaven must be!"

III. The City—Its Interior (Verses 22-27; 22: 1-5)

22 **And I saw no temple therein: for the Lord God the Almighty, and the Lamb, are the temple thereof.** 23 **And the city hath no need of the sun, neither of the moon, to shine upon it: for the glory of God did lighten it, and the lamp thereof is the Lamb.** 24 **And the nations shall walk amidst the light thereof: and the kings of the earth bring their glory into it.** 25 **And the gates thereof shall in no wise be shut by day (for there is no night there.)** Ordinarily, the gates of ancient cities were open during the day and closed at night; since there will be no night in the celestial city, the gates will never be closed. 26 **And they shall bring the glory and the honor of the nations into it:** 27 **and there shall in no wise enter into it anything unclean, or he that maketh an abomination and a lie: but only they that are written in the Lamb's book of life—**the family record, containing the names of God's children.

22: 1 **And he showed me a river of water of life, bright as crystal, proceeding out of the throne of God and of the Lamb,** 2 **in the midst of the street thereof. And on this side of the river and on that was the tree of life, bearing twelve manner of fruits, yielding its fruit every month: and the leaves of the tree were for the healing of the nations.** 3 **And there shall be no curse any more: and the throne of God and of the Lamb shall be therein: and his servants shall serve him;** 4 **and they shall see his face; and his n a m e shall be on their foreheads.** 5 **And there shall be night no more; and they need no light of lamp, neither of sun; for the Lord God shall give them light: and they shall reign for ever and ever.** When John looked within the city, what did he see? First, he saw no temple. The city itself is the holy of holies—hence, no need of a temple.

Why should there be a temple where God is so manifestly present? Second, a glorious system of illumination. (Verse 23.) Something brighter than the sun and the moon is shining therein—a light all-penetrating, never failing. In the holy city there are no dark places— of sin, of ignorance, of unbelief. Upon that fair city no night shall fall. Third, an ideal citizenship. (Verses 24-27.) The filth of old Jerusalem was carried outside the wall and burned, likewise, nothing that defiles shall be found in the new Jerusalem. All generations of the redeemed from every nation shall be gathered into the holy habitation. Fourth, a variety and an abundance of provisions. (Rev. 22: 1-5.) The water of life, like a stream in abundance, has its origin there. The tree of life, forfeited by sin (Gen. 3), with its variety of fruit and health-giving leaves, is there. And fifth, "there shall be no curse any more." No more curse of Satanic rule: for "the throne of God . . . shall be therein," etc. No more curse of loneliness: for "they shall see his face." No more curse of the beastly mark: for "his (God's) name shall be on their foreheads." No more curse of darkness: for night shall be no more —no more night of sin and sorrow, no more night of death and despair.

"In the land of fadeless day
Lies the city foursquare,
It shall never pass away,
And there is no night there."

From This Scripture Portion Learn:

1. That heaven is a new order, a new environment. "The first things are passed away." It is a place of "no mores"—no more tears. no more death, no more mourning, no more crying, no more pain.

2. The meaning of "the second death." The death of the body is due to Adam's sin; therefore it is inevitable; but the second death, "the lake of fire," comes as a consequence of man's own sin; therefore, it may be avoided.

3. That Jesus is not only "the light of the world" (John 8: 12), but also the light of heaven—"the lamp thereof is the Lamb." (See Isa. 60: 19. 20.)

4. That angels stand guard at the gates of pearl, admitting into the holy city all who are holy, and excluding all who are unholy.

For Class Discussion

1. What is the lesson subject?

2. What does the new Jerusalem represent?

3. Describe God's people—their origin, their adornment, their relationship with God.

4. What inheritance is promised to the one that overcomes?

5. In verse 8, what shall become of the people who do not overcome? What is the second death?

6. What did John see from a mountain great and high?

7. Give an exterior description of the new Jerusalem. Discuss: Its brightness; its security; its accessibility; its permanence; its perfection; its splendor.

8. Describe the interior of the city. Did John see a temple therein? Why? Discuss: Its system of illumination; its citizenship; the variety and abundance of its provisions; its immunity from the curse.

9. What practical lessons were suggested to you as you read this wonderful scripture portion? Quote the memory selection.

The Epilogue

As far as the unfolding of scenes of things to come is concerned, we closed the exposition of Revelation in the last paragraph. All that is now left is the Epilogue—the last word. Not only have we come to the final word of this particular book, but also of the Bible itself. It is with interest beyond the usual, therefore, that we approach the solemn words of the last assignment. In the verses before us we have an affirmation of the truthfulness of all that John had written on Patmos, Christ's words of warning and encouragement, and the final attestation of the book.

I. The Affirmation (Verses 6-9)

6 **And he**—probably "one of the seven angels" who had exhibited to John the vision of the new Jerusalem (Rev. 21: 9)—**said unto me, These words are faithful and true: and the Lord, the God of the spirits of the p r o p h e t s, sent his angel to show unto his servants the things which must shortly come to pass.** What John had heard while on Patmos had awed and overwhelmed him. They seemed too wonderful or too marvelous or too horrible to be true. The angel assured him of the truthfulness of all that had been spoken. The words were in harmony with unalterable facts and unchangeable principles. Therefore they could not pass away. (See Matt. 24: 35.) 7 **Behold, I come quickly,** said the Lord Jesus, confirming the declaration of the preceding verse. He will come quickly, to wind up the history of the present dispensation. We know not when. (See 2 Pet. 3: 8.) **Blessed is he that keepeth the words of the prophecy of this book.** He who keeps the words of the Lord is prepared for any contingency of life. (See Rev. 1: 3.)

8 **And I John am he that heard and saw these things,** i.e., the voices and visions that had come to him on the lonely isle. **And when I heard and saw I fell down to worship before the feet of the angel that showed me these things.** The beatifice vision overwhelmed him with reverential awe and he paid undue homage to the angel. On another occasion he had fallen into the same error (Rev. 19: 10), when he was similarly reproved. 9 **And he said unto me, See thou do it not: I am a fellow-servant with thee and with thy brethren the prophets.** In verse 6 we have "the spirits of the prophets," employed in much the same way. " 'The prophets' need not be restricted in meaning to either Old or New Testament prophets, but may include both." **And with them that keep the words of this book: worship God,** the true object of worship.

II. Christ's Words (Verses 10-15)

10 And he saith unto me, Seal not up the words of the prophecy of this book; for the time is at hand. The Revelation deals not merely with events far distant in the future, but also with those "at hand." Therefore, it was not a time of sealing, but of breaking seals, of proclaiming prophecy. Daniel (8: 26) was told to seal the vision, for the reason that it "belongeth to many days to come." **11 He that is unrighteous, let him do unrighteousness still; and he that is filthy, let him be made filthy still: and he that is righteous, let him do righteousness still: and he that is holy, let him be made holy still.** In eternity sin will be left to itself, righteousness to itself. "These words seem to be used ironically, as was sometimes the case with the prophet (cf. Ezek. 3: 27; 20: 39). The intention seems to be to stir men up to a realization of the nature of their conduct in continuing to reject the warnings of God." **12 Behold, I come quickly.** Be converted in the short time that remains, or be forever unconverted. **And my reward is with me, to render to each man according as his work is.** When the Lord comes in his glory, then will each man be found to have the thing for which he has striven. "The wages of sin" or "the gift of God"—each will be received in fulness. We shall reap what we sow. **13 I am the Alpha and the Omega, the first and the last, the beginning and the end.** In this expression, the Lord gives an affirmation of his eternal nature. (See Rev. 1: 8.) **14 Blessed are they that wash their robes,** in the blood of the Lamb that has been slain, **that they may have the right to come to the tree of life, and may enter in by the gates into the city.** This is the last beatitude of the Bible. As at the beginning of Jesus' ministry (Matt. 5), so at the close we find the word "blessed." To those who keep their garments unspotted (Jas. 1: 27; Rev. 2: 7), comes a twofold blessedness. First, the right to partake of the life-giving tree. This tree, forfeited through the disobedience of Adam (Gen. 3), may be regained by us through obedience to Christ. Second, an "abundant entrance" into the city of God (2 Pet. 1: 10, 11). **15 Without,** i.e., without the city. As a description of those within has been given, so now those without. All the souls who are outside this beautiful city are truly execrable. For outside the realm of blessedness **are the dogs** —the unclean and ravenous beasts of Eastern cities, types of vile and rapacious men. **And the sorcerers**—those who practice imposture in religion, who are skilled in the art of deception. **And the fornicators**— the dissolute and impure. **And the murderers**— private assassins, those who harbor hatred in their souls. (See 1 John 3: 15.) **And the idolators**— "Those who bow before the empty fashions of vanity, the parade of wealth, and the pomp and glitter of titled fools. Whatsoever in the human mind rules the soul is idolatry. There is only one true God and one true worship." **And every one that loveth and maketh** (or, doeth) **a lie**—the deceiver, those who deal in falsehood, in slander, in every form of deception.

III. The Final Attestation (Verses 16-21)

In these verses we have a series of last things, namely: The last invitation, the last warning, the past prayer, the last "Amen" and the last benediction.

16 I Jesus have sent mine angel to testify unto you these things for the churches. Thus, Jesus speaks to John, confirming the angelic testimony. **I am the root and the offspring of David, the bright, the morning star.** Jesus is "a shoot out of the stock of Jesse, and a branch out of his root" (Isa. 11: 1), the "Son, who was born of the seed of David according to the flesh" (Rom. 1: 3), the object of ancient prophecy, the long-promised and long-expected Messiah. He is "the bright, the morning star," the star which beams with its greatest brilliancy when the darkness is about to depart and the day is at hand. As "the root and offspring of David," he is connected with humanity; as "the bright, the morning star," he is connected with heaven.

17 And the Spirit and the bride say, Come. And he that heareth, let him say, Come. And he that is athirst, let him come: he that will, let him take the water of life freely. In this verse we have the last invitation. Notice: First, the ones who are inviting. The Spirit says, "Come" and is grieved when the call is slighted. The bride of the Lamb, the church, says, "Come." The one who hears is urged to "catch up the sound and pass it on." Second, the ones who are invited. "He that is athirst" is invited. Those who are painfully aware of the brevity of the life that now is and are athirst for a longer, fuller life, are invited. Those who are familiar with sorrow and long for the land of cloudless day, are invited. Those who are convicted of sin and thirst for purity and pardon are invited. (See John 4: 13, 14.) "He that will" is invited.

18 I testify unto every man that h e a r e t h the words of the prophecy of this book, If any man shall add unto them, God shall add unto him the plagues which are written in this book—the plagues of the seals (chapter 6), the plagues of the trumpets (chapters 8, 9 and 11), the plagues of the bowls (chapter 16), the doom of Babylon (chapter 18), etc. **19 And if any man shall take away from the words of the book of this prophecy, God shall take**

away his part from the tree of life, and out of the holy city, which are written in this book. (See Rev. 21: 1; 22: 5.) Just as the plagues are declared to be the portion of those who "add unto" the book, so those who "take away from the words" of the book shall be deprived of the blessings written in the book. This twofold warning is designed to guard the integrity of the book. (See Deut. 4: 2.)

20 He that testifieth these things saith, Yea: I come quickly. As the Revelation opens (1: 7), so it closes with this promise. This is an anchor and a stay of the saint, also the sound of alarm and a warning cry to the sinful. This is Jesus' last promise. We note with interest John's response. Amen: come, Lord Jesus. This is the last prayer of the Bible. Come, Lord Jesus and lift the burden. Come, Lord Jesus, and bring an end to all sin and sorrow. Come, Lord Jesus, and take us to thyself. There, let us abide.

21 The grace of the Lord Jesus be with the saints. Amen. This is the last benediction. The book closes, as it began, with grace. (See Rev. 1: 4.) God be with you.

From the Epilogue Learn:

1. That the words of this book are "faithful and true." This is the grand affirmation of the angel who revealed it, of Jesus who inspired it, of John who wrote it.

2. That upon all who keep the words of this book falls a blessedness.

3. That the Lord, not an angel and certainly not a man, should be the object of our worship and devotion.

4. That man should neither add to nor take from the word of God. Upon the ones who attempts to do so falls a curse.

5. That the Lord is coming not to set up an earthly reign, but to terminate all earthly affairs, to "render to each man according as his work is."

Memory Selection

"I am the root and offspring of David, the bright, the morning star." (Verse 16b.)

For Class Discussion

1. What is the subject of our lesson? What is the meaning of it?
2. Into what three parts may we divide the lesson text?

3. In verses 4-6, who affirms the truthfulness of the words of the book? In these verses, what promise does Jesus make? Upon whom is the state of blessedness pronounced? Was it right for John to worship an angel? It is right for us to worship an angel? a man?

4. Explain verses 10 and 11. What promise is given in verse 12? What blessing comes to the ones who wash their robes? Comment on verse 15.

5. Discuss the last things in verses 16-21.

6. What practical lessons are suggested by this scripture portion? Quote the memory selection.

.